New Mermaids

General editor: Brian Gibbons
Professor of English Literature, University of Münster

CHRISTOPHER MARLOWE

Dr Faustus

Edited by Roma Gill OBE

A & C BLACK • LONDON
W W NORTON • NEW YORK

Second edition 1989
Reprinted 1990, 1991, 1993, 1994, 1995, 1996, 1997, 1998, 2000,
2001(twice), 2002 (twice)

Printed with new cover 2003, 2004
A & C Black (Publishers) Limited
37 Soho Square, London W1D 3QZ
www.acblack.com

ISBN 0–7136–6790–7

First New Mermaid edition 1968

Published in the United States of America by
W. W. Norton & Company Inc.
500 Fifth Avenue, New York, N.Y. 10110

ISBN 0-393-90059-2

CIP catalogue records for this book are available
from the British Library and the Library of Congress

Printed in Great Britain by
Bookmarque Ltd, Croydon, Surrey

CONTENTS

IN MEMORY
OF
MY MOTHER

PREFACE

Nowadays it is generally recognised that plays, more than any other literary artefacts, are 'unstable'—that is to say, their texts are subject to constant revision and re-revision throughout their theatrical lives. Changes in personnel and politics have their effects on acting companies and, inevitably, on the plays that these produce. Alterations are made to texts, with or without—and sometimes in spite of—the dramatist's consent or even knowledge. The resignation of Edward Alleyn in 1602, and the censorious Act of Abuses in 1606, had remarkable consequences for *Dr Faustus*. There now exist *two* plays of this title! The later play, that represented by the B text of 1616, is not without interest and merit; but it must be recognised that the A text (1604), being less dilute, contains proportionately more of the work of Christopher Marlowe.

In 1964, when I started my work on *Dr Faustus*, it was still thought that the A text was merely an inferior version of the play more accurately presented in the B text. Consequently, the first New Mermaid edition (published in 1965) was based on B. This new edition is very different from its predecessor, but it offers, I believe, something more like the play that Marlowe wrote. The seventeenth-century additions, which were allowed to obscure the dramatist's design, have been removed to the Appendix. The resulting text is shorter and more dramatic; it is 'Elizabethan' rather than 'Jacobean'; and its meaning, although no simpler, is quite uncompromising. It is also a better play.   *October 1994*

INTRODUCTION

THE AUTHOR

At the age of twenty-nine Marlowe was murdered. His death was welcomed by Her Majesty's Privy Council, which later pardoned the murderer, and by certain popular moralists who hailed it as 'a manifest sign of God's judgement'[1] on a life of impiety and debauchery.

Marlowe was born into a turbulent Canterbury family. His father was a shoemaker of modest means and excessive pugnacity, while two of his sisters, Dorothy and Ann, were notorious in the town – the former for various trade and matrimonial intrigues, the latter a noted 'scold, common swearer and blasphemer of the name of God'.[2] Marlowe escaped from the family environment with the aid of those charitable Elizabethans who had endowed scholarships for the encouragement of learning in poor boys. The first scholarship, of £4 a year, took him to the King's School, Canterbury, from where he proceeded to Cambridge as a Matthew Parker scholar at Corpus Christi College. The Parker scholarship was awarded for three years in the first instance, and might be extended for a further three on evidence that the holder intended to take Holy Orders. Marlowe held his for the full six years. The College's Buttery Book shows him as an undergraduate whose expenditure easily exceeded his income but who from time to time spent nothing at all. There were, evidently, frequent and prolonged absences from Cambridge, and these gave the University cause to question his activities and to threaten, in 1587, to withold his final degree. But Marlowe had strings to pull. A letter from the Privy Council, with the overruling authority of, among others, Archbishop Whitgift, Sir Christopher Hatton, and Lord Burghley, explained in veiled hints the reason for these absences: Marlowe 'had done Her Majestic good service, and deserved to be rewarded for his faithfull dealinge'.[3] He probably went abroad – perhaps to visit the English Catholics at Rheims. Amidst much speculation one thing is clear: this 'good service' was not of the kind that is officially recorded and recognised.

A secret agent with an M.A. degree, Marlowe left Cambridge for London. There he consorted with playwrights, at one time sharing a room with Thomas Kyd, author of *The Spanish Tragedy*; quite possibly he associated also with the group of young intellectuals led by Sir Walter Raleigh. Although

[1] Thomas Beard, *Theatre of God's Judgements* (1597), ch. xxv
[2] See William Urry, 'Marlowe and Canterbury', *T.L.S.* (13 February 1964)
[3] Privy Council Register, xxix° Junij 1587; for a full documentation of Marlowe's life and death see J. Leslie Hotson, *The Death of Christopher Marlowe* (1925) and John Bakeless, *The Tragicall History of Christopher Marlowe* (Harvard, 1945)

the facts of his life are largely unknown, its tenor is certain. Arrested once on a charge of homicide, bound over at another time to keep the peace, Marlowe emerges from contemporary legal documents as a rash and fearless quarreller. Mario Praz calls him a *libertin*, using the word to mean both 'free-thinker' and, with its accumulated secondary meaning, 'man of loose morals'.[1] For the free-thinking there is ample evidence of surprising consistency. Richard Baines libelled Marlowe only a few days after the murder. The now famous libel[2] accuses the dramatist of blaspheming the Bible and mocking the state, reporting him as having said:

> ... That the first beginning of Religion was only to keep men in awe ...
> ... That Christ was a bastard and his mother dishonest ...
> ... that all the new testament is filthily written ...

and

> ... that he had as good Right to Coine as the Queen of England.

This last accusation is now supported by a recently-discovered letter from the governor of Flushing, which was sent to Lord Burghley in January 1602. It speaks of the involvement of Marlowe with Baines (who was a petty informer) and a goldsmith, and of an arrest at Flushing when Marlowe and the goldsmith were accused of 'coining'. But the governor, Robert Sidney, clearly has no faith in this charge:

> ... a dutch shilling was uttred, and els not any peece ... the metal is plain peuter and with half an ey to be discovered.[3]

Sir Robert cannot explain the presence of Marlowe in the Netherlands, or his relationship with Baines; but one obvious deduction is that Marlowe's shadowy connection with Her Majesty's secret service did not come to an end when he left Cambridge.

Baines continued his libel with the information that whatever the company he came into, Marlowe persuaded its members to atheism,

> Willing them not to be afeared of bugbears and hobgoblins, and utterly scorning both god and his ministers.

Marlowe sounds alternately like a perky undergraduate and like a man of plain common sense. But this is a twentieth-century view. To the Elizabethans,

---

[1] 'Christopher Marlowe', *E.S.*, XIII (1931)

[2] MS Harley 6648, ff. 185–6

[3] See R. B. Wernham, 'Christopher Marlowe at Flushing in 1592', *E.H.R.*, XCI (April, 1976), pp. 344–5

fearing for the sanctity of their church and the security of their state, these were 'monstruous opinions', menacing heresies. A warrant was issued for Marlowe's arrest, on evidence supplied perhaps by his former friend Kyd. Kyd himself had been arrested, accused of inciting mob violence and race riots against the Flemish protestants who were then settling in England. Under torture he broke down, and in two letters to Sir John Puckering, the Lord Keeper, he charged Marlowe with heresy and blasphemy.

Before the warrant could be executed Marlowe was killed. The inquest report tells of a squalid encounter in a Deptford tavern on 30 May 1593. Marlowe spent the day there with three 'gentlemen', talking and walking in the garden. But in the evening a quarrel was struck up over who should pay the bill, 'le recknynge', and in the scuffle that followed Marlowe drew his dagger and wounded one of his companions. The man, Ingram Frizar, snatched the weapon and

> in defence of his life, with the dagger aforesaid of the value of 12d. gave the said Christopher then & there a mortal wound over his right eye of the depth of two inches & of the width of one inch; of which mortal wound the aforesaid Christopher Morley then & there instantly died.[1]

The coroner's account puts a good face on the matter. Yet Ingram Frizar and one, if not both, of his accomplices had connections in some uncertain way with the secret service. Their past histories, and the speed with which, one month later, Frizar was granted a free pardon for the murder, suggest that the 'recknynge' settled in the Deptford tavern was an old score, and probably connected with Marlowe's secret service career.

Marlowe's contemporaries accepted the story of the brawl, but only one seems to have known its ostensible cause. Shakespeare's reference to Marlowe's death serves as an epitaph of his life, the brief life of his most brilliant colleague whose achievement, in five years, is second only to Shakespeare's own:

> A great reckoning in a little room
> *As You Like It*, III, iii, 11

THE PLAY

Date and Text

Marlowe's reputation rests on four great plays: *Tamburlaine* (in two parts), 1587–8; *The Jew of Malta*, 1590; *Edward II*, 1592; and *Dr Faustus*. At Cambridge

---

[1] Chancery Miscellanea, Bundle 64, File 8, No. 2416 (translated from the Latin)

Marlowe wrote translations of the Latin poets Lucan and Ovid, and also (perhaps) the early play Dido Queen of Carthage – which is a dramatic rendering (and translation) of Book VI of Virgil's *Aeneid*. Another play, *The Massacre at Paris*, was written at about the same time as *The Jew of Malta*: on a political and topical theme, it was popular in the theatre, but the mangled text in which it survives makes critical discussion almost impossible. A different work was *Hero and Leander*, an epic poem of great delight which seems to have been written late in Marlowe's short literary career and which is full of promise for a great future.

The proud-paced verse of *Tamburlaine* stormed the English stage. For his first public theme Marlowe took the story of a peasant warrior whose aspiring mind impelled him to conquest. Over a map of the world, drawn with detailed accuracy from Ortelius' *Theatrum Orbis Terrarum*, Marlowe played 'a great game of chess with kings and conquerors for pieces'.[1] Barabas, protagonist of *The Jew of Malta*, is the reverse of Tamburlaine; schemes of grandeur delight him less than grotesquely comic revenge plots to poison a whole convent of nuns. Far from striding across the known world in the majesty of power, he huddles in his counting-house, accumulating from all quarters of the globe 'Infinite riches in a little room'. King Edward lacks even this ambition, longing only for the 'nook or corner' which all England cannot afford where he may indulge his love for Gaveston. 'Marlowe's mighty line' (the description is Ben Jonson's[2]) is restrained in *Edward II*, but what seems like a loss in energy is compensated by a gain in human feeling.

None of Marlowe's plays can be dated with precision – and *Dr Faustus* is no exception. It had not been performed before the dramatist died in 1593; and although the Admiral's Men staged the other plays in the months immediately following the assassination (perhaps hoping to benefit from the publicity), *Dr Faustus* does not enter the repertoire until 30 September 1594, when the impresario Philip Henslowe recorded in his Diary[3] the fact that he had

> Rd at docter ffostose..iij^{h}xij^{s}.
>
> (p. 24)

The sum was large – greater than that taken at any other performance the same year; and further entries in the *Diary* testify to the play's continued popularity.

Dr Faustus remained unpublished until the seventeenth century – it was in the actors' own interests not to release the manuscript of their play

[1] Ethel Seaton, 'Marlowe's Map', *E & S, X* (1924), p. 35
[2] line 30 of his memorial verses to Shakespeare, published in the First Folio
[3] *Henslowe's Diary*, ed. R. A. Foakes and R. T. Rickert (1961)

to a publisher. On 7 January 1601 it was entered in the Stationers' Register:

> Tho. Busshell Entred for his copye under the handes. of Mr Docter Barlowe, and the Warden. A booke called the plaie of Doctor Faustus.

This, I suspect, was merely a 'blocking entry', giving notice of the printer's intention and not resulting immediately in an edition of the play. The first known edition is that of 1604, which was reprinted in 1609 and again in 1611; this is known as the A Text, to distinguish it from the very different B Text, an edition published in 1616 and reprinted several times thereafter. The titlepage of B2 (1619) advertises that the play is 'With new Additions' – a piece of information that ought to have been given three years earlier.

Marlowe's play was altered in 1602: Henslowe's *Diary* records the financial details:

> Lent unto the companye the 22 of november 1602
> to paye unto w^m Bvrde & Samwell Rowle   iiij^h
> for ther adicyones in docter fostes the some of
>
> (p. 206)

Such costly 'adicyones' must have been extensive. Perhaps Henslowe felt that *Dr Faustus*, although still a popular play, was somewhat old-fashioned in style, unsuited to modern – i.e. Jacobean – tastes. Furthermore, Henslowe's son-in-law and theatrical partner, the actor Edward Alleyn, was planning to leave the company. He had acted major roles such as Tamburlaine, Barabas, and Faustus; and he would not be easy to replace. A re-writing of the play would modernize it, and also add new interest to compensate for the loss of the leading performer. This is mere speculation, of course – an attempt to explain the problem created by the two texts of *Dr Faustus*.

The A Text, published in 1604
The B Text, published in 1616

B is not only longer and more diffuse than A; the play has also been subjected to severe censorship to satisfy a strict statute, the Act of Abuses, which became law in 1606:

> An Acte to restraine Abuses of Players
> ... That if at any tyme or tymes ... any person or persons doe or shall in any Stage play ... jestingly or prophanely speake or use the holy

Name of God or of Christ Jesus, or of the Holy Ghoste or of the
Trinitie, which are not to be spoken but with feare and reverence,
shall forfeite for everie such Offence by hym or them committed Tenne
Pounde.

The final soliloquy has lost much of its power in the B Text, where a wor-
ried Faustus has no vision of Christ's blood streaming in the firmament,
and thinks to 'leap up to heaven', rather than (like the A Faustus) 'to my
God'.

Until the middle of the twentieth century it was usual to accept the A
Text as being closer to Marlowe's original intention because closer in time
to his writing. But the efforts of certain scholars – notably Boas, Kirschbaum,
and Greg – succeeded in discrediting A as a 'Bad Quarto' (probably a
reporter's account of a shortened version of the play) and promoting the
B Text as a 'Good Quarto' (based, according to Greg, on Marlowe's 'foul
papers'). Greg's argument was ingenious and influential – but unnecessary:
there is very little wrong with the A Text, whereas B seems to be based on
a copy of A3 augmented by a theatrical manuscript which has been 'edited'
by a book-keeper, censored in accordance with the Act of Abuses, and altered
by the two dramatists referred to in Henslowe's *Diary*.

The present edition, then, takes A as its copy-text; readings from B are
accepted when all of the surviving impressions of A (1604, 1609, and 1611)
are manifestly deficient or erroneous.

But what kind of MS was printer's copy for the A Text? Sixteen months
elapsed between the dramatist's death and the appearance of his play on the
stage – and I suggest that so much time was needed to find some way of
completing Marlowe's unfinished work. Some of *Dr Faustus* – the beginning
and the end – is in Marlowe's finest style. The mighty line echoes through
the first and last soliloquies; it is heard again in the Scholars' praise of Helen
and Faustus' own apostrophe to the vision. But the comedy does not seem
to be that of the author of *The Jew of Malta* and *The Massacre at Paris*, whose
humour is cool, witty, and even cruel. The Prologue to Part 1 of *Tamburlaine*
was scornful of contemporary theatrical practice and the crude 'conceits that
clownage keeps in pay' – but such 'conceits', the stock-in-trade of Elizabethan
clowns, occupy the central scenes of *Dr Faustus* and bridge the twenty-four
year gap between the signing of the infernal contract and its expiry date.

Perhaps Marlowe was not interested in the central part of the narrative
which was the source for his play; certainly the episodes become repetitive
and tedious as the *Faustbook* degenerates into a collection of jests inter-
spersed with moralizing tracts. The comic scenes in the play, however, are
not all of a piece. Scenes 2 and 4 appear to be the work of some university

wit – perhaps Thomas Nashe – who develops the featureless choric presenter of the Prologue into the character of Wagner. Wagner is allowed almost a solo performance before the bewildered Scholars, but when he attempts to imitate Faustus and enrol the Clown in his service, it is the Clown who takes possession of the scene, demonstrating different comedy routines which were stock dramatic numbers – the conceits of clownage. The actor who played the Clown in *Dr Faustus* must also have had the role of the clown, known as Adam, in *A Looking Glass for London*, written by Lodge and Greene, and entered in the Stationers' Register in March 1594: he freely transposed lines between this play and *Dr Faustus*. In *A Looking Glass* the Clown, threatened by the devil, attacks with his 'cudgell' until the devil pleads for mercy, when Adam boasts

> Then I may count my selfe I thinke a tall man, that am able to kill a diuell. Now who dare deale with me in the parish, or what wench in *Ninivie* will not loud me, when they say, there goes he that beate the diuell.
>
> G3ᵛ

The lines are introduced into *Dr Faustus* (Scene 4) when Wagner invokes the devils to threaten his reluctant servant, but now the Clown only entertains the possibility of beating the devil: since the lines do not arise directly out of the dramatic situation, it is certain that Marlowe's play must be the borrower.

The *Looking Glass* lines were not the Clown's only contribution. It is very tempting to identify this character with the comic actor, John Adams, who played with Sussex's Men in 1576, and with The Queen's Men in 1583 and 1588.[1] His reputation was good enough to link him with Richard Tarlton in the memory of the Stage-keeper in Jonson's *Bartholmew Fair* when he remembers how

> Adams, the rogue, ha' leaped and capered upon him [Tarlton], and ha' dealt his vermin about as though they had cost him nothing.
>
> (Induction, ll. 38–40)

Adams must have been the sort of clown who relied upon a single gimmick– having 'one sute of jeasts, as a man is known by one sute of Apparell' (Q1 *Hamlet*, III,ii). Adams' 'sute of jeasts' – the stage business with fleas – served unusually well for *Dr Faustus*, where the Clown's familiar vermin ('as bold with my flesh as if they had paid for my meat and drink') – enact the diabolic threat to Faustus: 'If thou repent, devils will tear thee in pieces'.

---

[1] Cf. E. K. Chambers, *Elizabethan Stage* (1923), ii, 296

The Source

THE
HISTORIE
of the damnable
life, and deserved death of
Doctor John Faustus,
Newly imprinted, and in conveni-
ent places imperfect matter amended:
according to the true Copie printed
at Franckfort, *and translated into*
English by P. F. *Gent.*[1]

Stories of witchcraft and enchantment, wandering loose in men's minds, attached themselves in the early sixteenth century to a real-life Georg or Johannes Faustus, scholar and reputed magician of no fixed abode. After this man's death – which gave rise to the most fantastic story of all – his fabled doings were assembled in a 'biography' published in Frankfurt in 1587. The book caught the eye of an Englishman and, translated, was an immediate success. Nothing, not even the name, is known of the transla- tor, P. F. *Gent.* Whoever he was, P. F. shared the German author's staunchly protestant outlook. At some time, however, he must have toured Italy, and because of his efforts to turn the pious jestbook into a Blue Guide we can be certain that Marlowe used the English translation and not the German original. The German, for instance, makes only passing reference to Venice, whereas P. F. remarks the Piazza San Marco and 'the sumptuous Church standing therein called Saint *Markes*'. Marlowe even adds a further detail, although this must be supplied only from his own imagination:

> In midst of which a sumptuous temple stands,
> That threats the stars with her aspiring top.

More intelligent than either of his predecessors, Marlowe had more respect for his hero. No longer the conjuror and calendar-maker of the source, this Faustus is a scholar of distinction. Marlowe's own learning went to the creation of his protagonist, and the verse of the play is heavily encrusted with references to texts that the Cambridge undergraduate must have studied.

Marlowe's source is the subject of a sensitively imaginative study by William Empson, *Faust and the Censor* (1987).

[1] British Museum, C.27.b.43

The Tragedy

The Tragical History
of
the life and death
of
DR FAUSTUS

Boundless in its aspirations, unceasing in its compulsions, the Renaissance mind is the theme of all Marlowe's plays:

> Our souls, whose faculties can comprehend
> The wondrous architecture of the world,
> And measure every wand'ring planet's course,
> Still climbing after knowledge infinite,
> And always moving as the restless spheres,
> Wills us to wear ourselves and never rest ...
>
> *1 Tamburlaine*, II,vii, 21–6

Dr Faustus, the first figure on the English stage who deserves to be called a character, is the epitome of Renaissance aspiration. He has all the divine discontent, the unwearied and unsatisfied striving after knowledge that marked the age in which Marlowe wrote. An age of exploration, its adventurers were not only the merchants and seamen who sailed round the world, but also the scientists, astronomers who surveyed the heavens with their 'optic glass', and those scholars who travelled in the realms of gold to bring back tales of a mighty race of gods and heroes in ancient Greece and Rome. The first soliloquy is 'no mere reckoning of accounts but an inventory of the Renaissance mind'.[1] Faustus is one of the new men. For him, as for Marlowe, lowly birth was no bar to a university education; and as he sits alone in his study reading from the Latin textbooks, he is linked in a common language with scholars from Oxford, Cambridge, and all over the civilized world. Rhetoric, jurisprudence, and medicine have trained a mind apt for questioning, eager for learning, and reluctant to take on trust even the most elementary facts, let alone those hypotheses incapable of empirical proof. The Faustus who refuses to accept from Mephastophilis the evidence for hell's existence is true to himself. His pitiful shortsightedness is all too evident, but there is also a determination to believe only what he himself can prove. This has made him the distinguished scholar he is, the

---

[1] Harry Levin, *Christopher Marlowe: the Overreacher* (1954, 2nd ed. 1965), p. 134

man whose triumphant cry '*sic probo*' has echoed his fame through the German universities. Men of Faustus' calibre were not unknown to Marlowe's age. They were valuable, and they were dangerous. Representative were Sir Walter Raleigh and his friends, meeting together to discuss philosophy, to debate religion, and to gaze at the stars through Thomas Heriot's new telescope. They attracted much unwanted attention, with accusations of witchcraft and devil-worship. James VI, piously warning his Scottish subjects against the deceits of the devil, observed that those attracted to black magic were, more often than not, men

> having attained to a great perfection in learning, & yet remaining overbare (alas) of the spirit of regeneration and frutes thereof: finding all naturall things common, aswell to the stupid pedants as unto them, they assaie to vendicate unto them a greater name, by not onlie knowing the course of things heavenlie, but likewise to clim to the knowledge of things to come thereby.
>
> *Daemonologie* (Edinburgh, 1597), p. 10

The more man discovered about the universe and his place in it, the more imperative it became for Authority to stress the dangers inherent in the pursuit of knowledge. The wrath of the Almighty and the threat of eternal damnation were powerful deterrents.

The soliloquy with which the play opens should not be read as the random notions of a single idle moment; rather, it is the utterance of thoughts that have been formulating for years in Faustus' mind. He stands at the frontiers of knowledge. The whole of Renaissance learning is within his grasp, but on closer scrutiny of the parts the whole crumbles away and he is left with nothing but a handful of dust. Nothing in the great university curriculum can overcome the melancholy fact – 'Yet art thou still but Faustus, and a man' (Scene 1, line 23). Faustus shares with Hamlet, equally a product of Wittenberg scepticism, this perception of man's paradoxical nature:

> What a piece of work is a man! how noble in reason! how infinite in faculties! . . . the beauty of the world, the paragon of animals! And yet, to me, what is this quintessence of dust?
>
> *Hamlet*, II, ii, 293–7

It is this that gives rise to the irony that is the characteristic mode of the play: Faustus begins by longing to be more than human; he ends by imploring metamorphosis into the sub-human. Incidental ironies have a sharp impact within this structure – as when Faustus seals his deed of blood with the last words of Christ on the cross: '*Consummatum est*' (Scene 5, line 74). The impassioned appeal

> Ah Christ my Saviour, seek to save
> Distressed Faustus' soul
>
> Scene 5, lines 257–8

is answered by the emergence of the infernal trinity looking, as J. B. Steane comments, like 'the party bosses in a totalitarian state before one guilty of thought-crime'.[1] Certain words, frequently reiterated, carry an ambivalence that points to this initial paradox. Both *cunning* and *conceit* were at a semantic crossroads when Marlowe wrote. The translator of the Psalms could write, for the Authorized Version, 'If I forget thee, O Jerusalem, let my right hand forget her cunning' (Ps. 137) at much the same time as Bacon gave the definition 'We take cunning for a sinister and crooked wisdom'.[2] Marlowe plays delicately with both meanings, often balancing the older usage against the newer:

> Till, swollen with cunning, of a self conceit.
>
> Prologue, line 20

Neither *cunning* nor *conceit*, however, has the force Marlowe can give to the simple word *man*. Faustus envisages a world of power and delight which 'Stretcheth as far as doth the mind of man' (Scene 1, line 61). Human potential is set against human limitation in a single word. It is to redeem himself, by his own efforts, from this paradox that Faustus turns longing eyes on the magic books that will make him 'a mighty god' – and ultimately damn him for ever.

Dr Faustus is a tragedy of damnation. In his source Marlowe found the story of a scholar who gave his soul to the devil in return for twenty-four years of knowledge and pleasure. The rewards were miserably inadequate, and are shown as such in the play, where Faustus is seen as a spectator at a conventional masque of the Seven Deadly Sins; as an astronaut circling the world; as a common illusionist entertaining at a Royal Command performance; and as a mystical greengrocer contenting a pregnant duchess with out-of-season grapes. Some critics, like Warren D. Smith, claim that the trivialities of the middle parts of the play show Marlowe intent on

---

[1] J. B. Steane, *Marlowe* (1965), p. 141
[2] *Essays*, 'Of Cunning'

'establishing evil, though terrible in consequence, as actually petty in nature'.[1] On such a reading one can trace a gradual deterioration in the character of the protagonist:

> From a proud philosopher, master of all human knowledge, to a trickster, to a slave of phantoms, to a cowering wretch: that is a brief sketch of the progress of Dr Faustus.[2]

Robert Ornstein, however, sees no such deterioration in Dr Faustus, arguing that the scholar 'grows more gracious'[3] as he approaches his catastrophe; and Clifford Leech finds that

> Faustus's moment of highest authority, the moment when he is nearest to freedom, is not when he signs the bond but when he addresses the shape of Helen and puts himself into hell.[4]

Perhaps every critic creates his *own* Faustus, interpreting 'Dr Faustus' – both the play and its eponymous hero – according to his personal experience and philosophy!

Even so, the interpretation must be based on an attempt to understand Marlowe's position, and some of the ideas which he shared with the Elizabethan audiences – whose approval of the play is vouched by the box-office receipts recorded in Henslowe's *Diary*.

Quarrelsome, violent, homosexual, a mocking atheist – this is the Marlowe of contemporary scandal, and the one who is best known today. But before this came the holder of the Archbishop Parker scholarship, the Cambridge student of divinity who – from the evidence of this last play – studied the theological texts in the library of Corpus Christi as avidly and earnestly as his Faustus promises to read Lucifer's presentation volume. Evidence of this is in Mephastophilis' account of the torments of deprivation:

> Think'st thou that I, who saw the face of God,
> And tasted the eternal joys of heaven,
> Am not tormented with ten thousand hells
> In being deprived of everlasting bliss!

Scene 3, lines 78–81

---

[1] 'The Nature of Evil in *Dr Faustus*', *M.L.R.*, LX (April, 1965), p. 171

[2] Helen Gardner, 'The Tragedy of Damnation', *Elizabethan Drama*, ed. R. J. Kaufmann (New York, 1961), p. 321

[3] Robert Ornstein, 'Marlowe and God: The Tragic Theology of *Dr Faustus*', *PMLA*, LXXXIII (1968)

[4] Clifford Leech, *Christopher Marlowe: Poet for the Stage* (New York, 1986), p. 98

The notion is not that of *EFB*, nor does it come from Marlowe's own imagination: the words are directly translated from the Latin of St John Chrysostom (see note p. 41). Just before this Faustus, refusing to distinguish between the Christian hell and the pagan Elysium, proposes for himself an eternity among the Greek philosophers in the words of Averroes (see note p. 40). Marlowe the theologian has at least as great a part in this play as Marlowe the rebel.

Faustus takes his first step along the primrose path when he sets material benefits before spiritual blessings. Contemplating magic, anticipating its rewards with Valdes and Cornelius, he promises himself all the glory and riches of the Renaissance world. From Mephastophilis he demands to 'live in all voluptuousness' (Scene 3, line 93). Even before he succumbs to the lure of magic, his mind has been tempted by thoughts of wealth: 'Be a physician, Faustus, heap up gold' (Scene 1, line 14). Yet although this obsession with luxury is a flaw in the nature of one dedicated to the search for knowledge, its seriousness must not be magnified until it obscures the real issues. In the first soliloquy Faustus rejects the study of law, leaving it to the 'mercenary drudge Who aims at nothing but external trash' (Scene 1, lines 34–5); all the gold that the doctor can heap up will not reconcile him to the limitations of medical skill, through whose aid he can restore only health, not life.[1] And when, in an early agony of indecision, he weighs the profit and the loss, it is not riches that he puts into the opposite scale:

> Have not I made blind Homer sing to me
> Of Alexander's love, and Oenon's death?
> And hath not he that built the walls of Thebes
> With ravishing sound of his melodious harp,
> Made music with my Mephastophilis?
>
> Scene 5, lines 202–6

With the help of magic he has gained entry into another world, later to be represented in the form of Helen of Troy, whose value far exceeds the riches of all the Venetian argosies, Indian gold, and Orient pearl.

The process of damnation begins with the signing of the pact. Greg[2] was the first critic to take serious notice of the first article in the infernal contract: 'that Faustus may be a spirit in form and substance' (Scene 5, line 96). To

---

[1] Christopher Ricks discusses the importance of the medical skill in a plague-ridden England in '*Doctor Faustus* and Hell on Earth', *E & S*, XXXV, No. 2 (April, 1985), pp. 101–120

[2] The Damnation of Faustus', *M.L.R.*, XLI (1946)

the Elizabethans, *spirit* used in this way could mean only 'devil', and by assuming diabolic nature Faustus, in the eyes of the orthodox, would be instantly damned. Lucifer and all the fallen angels were beyond the reach of God's mercy; although God still had power to forgive, they lacked the capacity to repent and *receive* forgiveness. Aquinas is the chief authority here, and his doctrine, expounded in *Summa Theologica* i, 64, is echoed to the letter in one of Donne's sermons:

> To those that fell, can appertain no reconciliation; no more then to those that die in their sins; for *Quod homini mors, Angelis casus*; The fall of the Angels wrought upon them, as the death of a man does upon him.
>
> *LXXX Sermons* (1640), p. 9

To Lucifer, with his legalistic turn of mind, the contract is binding:

> Christ cannot save thy soul, for he is just.
> There's none but I have interest in the same.
>
> Scene 5, lines 259–60

The Evil Angel is similarly insistent, telling Faustus flatly

> Thou art a spirit, God cannot pity thee.
>
> Scene 5, line 189

The play would have stopped at this point, so far as the tragic part is concerned, had Faustus, the Good Angel, and Marlowe himself shared Lucifer's opinion as to the irrevocability of the compact. But there is still hope in the Good Angel's comforting words: 'Faustus repent, yet God will pity thee' (Scene 5, line 188). By signing the bond with its ominous first clause Faustus is not cut off from forgiveness; but the effects of his sin, in turning away from God, make it virtually impossible for him to accept the offered mercy. Repentance is all that is needed, yet to his dismay he find 'My heart's so hardened I cannot repent' (Scene 5, line 194).

The devils are adept at pricking the bubble of human self-glorification, and Faustus' pride is punctured in his first encounter with Mephastophilis. Soaring, as he thinks, to the height of his powers as 'conjuror laureate', he is jolted sharply back to earth by the fiend's casual admission that the conjuring was of no real import: 'I came now hither of mine own accord' (Scene 3 line 45). Hell's rewards are as the Dead Sea apples to Milton's fallen angels: mere ashes in his mouth. Repeated questioning of Mephastophilis brings no satisfaction; the devil can tell him only what he already knows and, forbidden to speak the praise of God, cannot give him the answer he wants to hear:

> FAUSTUS   Tell me who made the world?
> MEPHASTOPHILIS
> I will not.

Scene 5, lines 241–2

His pride dashed, Faustus becomes increasingly aware of the emptiness of his bargain and the reality of damnation. The pride with which this Renaissance superman scorned his human nature and aspired to become 'a mighty god' leads him inevitably to its opposite, despair; and from this there is no salvation.

There are some sins on which God will have no mercy; although He will forgive violation of the decalogue, and even blasphemy against Christ, yet

> whosoever speaketh against the Holy Ghost, it shall not be forgiven him, neither in this world, neither in the world to come.

Matthew xii, 32

The precise nature of the sin against the Holy Ghost, not defined in the Gospel, has always exercised theologians: but Renaissance thinkers generally agreed that pride and despair, inextricably linked, must be so called. The 'Schoolemen', writes Donne, have noted certain sins

> which they have called sins against the Holy Ghost, because naturally they shut out those meanes by which the Holy Ghost might work upon us. The first couple is, *presumption* and *desperation*; for presumption takes away the fear of God, and desperation the love of God . . . And truly . . . To presume upon God, that God cannot damn me eternally in the next world, for a few half-houres in this . . . Or to despair, that God will not save me . . . al these are shrewd and slippery approaches towards the sin against the Holy Ghost.

LXXX Sermons, pp. 349–50

The play ends where it began, in the solitude of Faustus' study, and it is here that Faustus finally damns himself, although for a moment, just after the Old Man's speech, he comes very close to repentance and salvation.

The Old Man comes, like the personification of Mercy in the Morality Play *Mankind* who rescues the protagonist from worldly snares, to advise Faustus that there is still a chance that he will be saved from eternal damnation. The man who has abjured the Scriptures, forsaken God, and trafficked with the devil, can still implore

> mercy, Faustus, of thy saviour sweet,
> Whose blood alone must wash away thy guilt.
>
> Scene 12, lines 36–7

But hell's present physical tortures terrify him more than the thought of future damnation, and instead of withstanding the momentary agony (as the Old Man will do later) Faustus requests instead the comfort of

> That heavenly Helen which I saw of late,
> Whose sweet embracings may extinguish clean
> These thoughts that do dissuade me from my vow.
>
> Scene 12, lines 75–7

Helen of Troy, twice passing over the stage, pausing for one brief moment yet speaking nothing, is the key figure in *Dr Faustus*. For this, Faustus has sold his soul. All the glory that was Greece was embodied, for the Renaissance, in this woman; her story was the story in brief of another world, superhuman and immortal. Helen's first appearance to the Scholars is no accident, no mere matter of a dramatist making double use of a bright idea. After their single appearance (Scene 2) at the beginning of the play the Scholars seem to have been forgotten; but this scene has shown them to be men of moderate awareness, eminently sensible and a little humourless. Their comments on the apparition (Scene 12, lines 16–24) equip us to judge for ourselves when it is seen again. Helen is the 'only paragon of excellence' in the eyes of these sober men, and their ordinary understanding is 'Too simple . . . to tell her praise'. The second appearance, attended by two Cupids and heralded, we must assume, by the music directed for the earlier entrance, has a ritual solemnity. This, and the formal ordering of Faustus' speech, mark the episode as what T. S. Eliot would have called 'a moment in and out of time'.[1] Faustus breaks the silence with the awed amazement of some of Marlowe's finest lines:

> Was this the face that launched a thousand ships,
> And burnt the topless towers of Ilium?
>
> Scene 12, lines 81–2

---

[1] *Four Quartets*, 'Little Gidding'

Declaring his devotion, he is exalted to heroic stature and promises vigorous action in verse of soaring energy which comes to rest at last on Helen's lips:

> And then return to Helen for a kiss.
>
> Scene 12, line 93

The speech is a rapture of applause – for Helen herself, for the eternal beauty of form, for all the glory that defies and withstands the canker of Time. But it is more than this. As the delighted verse surges forward to praise what is lovely and enduring, an undertow drags back to remind us that this beauty brought destruction: a city was burnt, topless towers laid in the dust. In the stillness of a single couplet the two movements are balanced:

> Brighter art thou than flaming Jupiter
> When he appeared to hapless Semele.
>
> Scene 12, lines 96–7

Semele, despite repeated warnings, persisted in her demands to see her lover in all his splendour. But the sight of Jupiter's divine majesty was greater than mortal eyes could bear to look upon, and the 'hapless Semele' was consumed by the glory. Helen has all of Jupiter's terrible burning beauty – and Faustus is damned by the vision. This is no mere fancy of Marlowe's, powerful though such a fancy would be. That which appears as Helen is no more the woman herself than the apparition which so pleased the German emperor was indeed Alexander. Faustus sees a spirit, a devil, in the form of Helen and, forgetful of his admonitions to the emperor, he speaks to it and touches it. Helen's lips 'suck forth' his soul in more than metaphor. The kiss signals the ultimate sin, demoniality, the bodily intercourse with spirits.[1] Now the Old Man gives up hope of saving Faustus. After such knowledge there is no forgiveness.

The last soliloquy reverses the first. The proud scholar who had fretted at the restrictions imposed by the human condition and longed for the immortality of a god now seeks to avoid an eternity of damnation. Like a trapped animal he lashes out against the mesh he has woven for himself, and becomes more entangled. To be physically absorbed, to be 'a creature wanting soul', 'some brutish beast', even, at the last, to be no more than 'little water drops' – this is the final hope of the pride of Wittenberg. Time is the dominant in this speech. The measured regularity of the opening

---

[1] First pointed out by Greg in the essay referred to above

gives way to a frantic tugging in two directions as Faustus suffers the opposing forces of Christ and Lucifer:

> O I'll leap up to my God! Who pulls me down?
>
> Scene 13, line 71

The pace and the passion increase as the clock strikes relentlessly, and the second half-hour passes more quickly than the first. We are agonizingly aware of the last minutes of Faustus' life, trickling through the hour-glass with what seems like ever-increasing speed. But as each grain falls, bringing Faustus closer to his terrible end, we become more and more conscious of the deserts of vast eternity and damnation that open up beyond death. When Macbeth or Lear dies the tragedy is ended with a final harmonious chord, but the discords of Faustus' last lines cannot be easily resolved.

Dr Faustus has much in common with the late medieval Morality Plays; but there is much that is different. The eponymous heroes of *Mankind* and *Everyman* are, like Faustus, tempted to sin; and they fall. But, counselled by the representations of Mercy and Knowledge, they recognize the error of their ways, repent, and are redeemed. Faustus, however, finding his heart 'so hardened [he] cannot repent', is in a worse dilemma than his predecessors – perhaps because he is more intelligent and individual than them. John Donne's Sonnet IV articulates the problem:

> Yet grace, if thou repent, thou canst not lack;
> But who shall give thee that grace, to begin?

Marlowe's sympathies (if the energy of the verse means anything at all) are for the rebel, who is impeded in his pursuit of science and frustrated in his efforts to assert his individuality. But he also feels deeply for the bleakly unhappy Mephastophilis, who is possessed of all the knowledge that Faustus desires, and who is 'tormented with ten thousand hells' because he has forfeited the 'everlasting bliss' that the doctor is so ready to part with.

FURTHER READING

Bevington, David, *From 'Mankind' to Marlowe* (Harvard, 1962)

Bowers, Fredson, 'Marlowe's *Dr Faustus*: the 1602 Additions', *Studies in Bibliography* 26 (1973)

Brockbank, J. P., *Marlowe; 'Dr Faustus'* (1962)

Cartwright, Kent, *Theatre and Humanism*, (Cambridge, 1999)

Cole, Douglas, *Suffering and Evil in the Plays of Christopher Marlowe* (1964)

Cole, Douglas, *Christopher Marlowe and the Renaissance of Tragedy* (Westport, Conn., and London, 1995)

Downie, J. A. and J. T. Parnell, eds. *Constructing Christopher Marlowe*, (Cambridge, 2000)

Empson, William, *Faustus and the Censor: The English Faustbook and Marlowe's 'Dr Faustus'*, ed. John Henry Jones (Oxford: Blackwell, 1987)

Grantley, Darryll and Roberts, Peter (eds), *Christopher Marlowe and English Renaissance Culture* (Aldershot, 1996)

Greg, W. W., 'The Damnation of Faustus', *M.L.R.*, XLI (1946)

Hopkins, Lisa, *Christopher Marlowe: A Literary Life* (Macmillan, 2000)

Jones, John Henry (ed), *The English Faust Book* (1994)

Jump, John (ed.), *Marlowe: 'Dr Faustus' – a casebook* (1969)

Leech, Clifford, *Christopher Marlowe: poet for the stage* (New York, 1986)

Levin, Harry, *The Overreacher* (1954)

McAlindon, T., '*Doctor Faustus*: The Predestination Theory', *English Studies* 76 (May 1995), 215–20

Pechter, Edward, *What Was Shakespeare? Renaissance Plays and Changing Critical Practice* (Ithaca: Cornell University Press, 1995)

Pettitt, T., 'The Folk-Play in Marlowe's *Dr Faustus*', *Folklore* 9:1 (1980)

Rasmussen, Eric, *A Textual Companion to Dr Faustus* (1993)

Ricks, Christopher, '*Dr Faustus* and Hell on Earth', *Essays in Criticism*, XXXV, No. 3 (April; 1985)

Roberts, Gareth, 'Necromantic Books: Christopher Marlowe, Doctor Faustus and Agrippa of Nettesheim', in Grantley, Darryll & Roberts, Peter (eds), *Christopher Marlowe and English Renaissance Culture* (Hants: Scolar, 1996), 148–71

Sales, Roger, *Christopher Marlowe* (Houndmills, Basingstoke and London: Macmillan, 1991)

Sanders, Wilbur, *The Dramatist and the Received Idea* (1968)

Smith, Robert A. H., 'Marlowe and Peele: The Final Scholar Scene in *Faustus* B Text', *Notes and Queries* 47 (2000) pp. 40–42

Steane, J. B., *Marlowe: a critical study* (1964)

Sullivan, Ceri, 'Faustus and the Apple', *Review of English Studies: A Quarterly Journal of English Literature and the English Language* 47:185 (Feb. 1996), 47–52

ABBREVIATIONS

I have followed the usual practice in referring to the seventeenth-century editions of *Dr Faustus*: 'A' indicates substantial agreement between all the A Texts, which are referred to separately on occasion as A1 (1604), A2 (1609), and A3 (1611); the B texts (1616, 1619, 1620, 1624, 1628, and 1631) are similarly distinguished. Modern editions are referred to as follows:

Boas   *The Tragical History of Doctor Faustus,* edited by F. S. Boas (1932)

Bullen   *The Works of Christopher Marlowe,* edited by A. H. Bullen (1885)

Dyce   *The Complete Works of Christopher Marlowe,* edited by A. Dyce (1850)

Greg   *Marlowe's Dr Faustus' 1604-1616: Parallel Texts,* edited by W. W. Greg (1950)

Jump   *Dr Faustus,* edited by John D. Jump (1962)

Other works frequently referred to are:

EFB   *The English Faust Book,* the name given to Marlowe's source [*The Historic of the damnable life, and deserved death of Doctor Iohn Faustus,* translated by P. F. (1592)]

Kocher   P. H. Kocher, *Christopher Marlowe* (Chapel Hill,1946)

Names of periodicals are abbreviated:

E.L.H.   *English Literary History*

E.S.   *English Studies*

E & S   *Essays and Studies*

M.L.N.   *Modern Language Notes*

M.L.Q.   *Modern Language Quarterly*

M.L.R.   *Modern Language Review*

N & Q   *Notes and Queries*

P.Q.	*Philological Quarterly*
R.E.S.	*Review of English Studies*
T.L.S.	*Times Literary Supplement*

Quotations from other plays by Marlowe are taken from *The Plays of Christopher Marlowe*,' edited by Roma Gill (1971); those from Shakespeare's plays are from the Riverside edition.

THE 6
TRAGICALL
History of D. Faustus.

As it hath bene Acted by the Right
Honorable the Earle of Nottingham his servants.

Written by Ch. Marl.

LONDON
Printed by V.S. for Thomas Bushell. 1604.

The printer's device on the titlepage is McKerrow 142; it is described as 'A boy with wings upon his right arm and with his left hand holding, or fastened to, a weight', the emblem signifying talent frustrated by poverty. It was not unique to *Dr Faustus*: the printer, Simmes, had used it on several other books, including the 1597 quarto of Shakespeare's *Richard II*
(*Photo: Bodleian Library, Oxford*)

[DRAMATIS PERSONAE

Chorus

Dr John Faustus

Wagner *his servant, a student*

Valdes
Cornelius ⎫ *his friends, magicians*

Three Scholars

The Good Angel

The Evil Angel

Mephastophilis

Lucifer

Belzebub

Old Man

The Clown
Robin ⎫
Rafe ⎭ *ostlers at an inn*

Vintner

Horse-courser

The Pope
The Cardinal of Lorraine

Mephastophilis This version of the character's name is used consistently throughout the A Text; the B Text spelling, 'Mephostophilis', is used in the Appendix of scenes from that text. William Empson has a note on the various spellings in *Faustus and the Censor* (1987), pp. 45–6*n*

The Emperor Charles V

A Knight *at the emperor's court*

Duke of Vanholt

Duchess of Vanholt

Spirits presenting
The Seven Deadly Sins
Pride
Covetousness
Wrath
Envy
Gluttony
Sloth
Lechery

Alexander the Great and his Paramour

Helen of Troy

Attendants, Friars, and Devils]

Dr Faustus

PROLOGUE

Enter CHORUS

CHORUS

    Not marching now in fields of Thrasimene,
    Where Mars did mate the Carthaginians,
    Nor sporting in the dalliance of love,
    In courts of kings where state is overturned,
    Nor in the pomp of proud audacious deeds,   5
    Intends our Muse to vaunt his heavenly verse:
    Only this (Gentlemen) we must perform,
    The form of Faustus' fortunes good or bad.
    To patient judgements we appeal our plaud,
    And speak for Faustus in his infancy: 10
    Now is he born, his parents base of stock,
    In Germany, within a town called Rhodes;
    Of riper years to Wittenberg he went,
    Whereas his kinsmen chiefly brought him up.
    So soon he profits in divinity,   15
    The fruitfull plot of scholarism graced,
    That shortly he was graced with doctor's name,

---

s.d   *Chorus* Marlowe uses a single figure (subsequently identified with Wagner) to introduce
      the play and link the dramatic episodes; the 'Chorus' here fulfils the function of the
      'Doctor' or presenter, of the Morality Plays
1–5   The Prologue speaks of plays already performed, but – whether these were written by
      Marlowe or merely part of the company's repertoire – the references are unclear.
      There is no trace of any play showing the victory of the Carthaginians under Hannibal
      at Lake Thrasymenus in 217 B.C.; and any number of plays (including Marlowe's own
      Edward II) could be said to show 'the dalliance of love' in royal courts
  2 *Mars* the Roman god of war
     mate ally himself with
  3 *dalliance* frivolity
  6 *our Muse* our poet; the Chorus is speaking on behalf of the acting company
     vaunt B (daunt A) show off
  9 *appeal our plaud* ask for applause
 12 *Rhodes* Roda, since 1922 Stadtroda (in Germany)
 13 *Wittenberg* Hamlet's university, and Luther's, was the home of scepticism; but this
      Wittenberg is, in all outward appearances, Marlowe's own Cambridge
 14 *Whereas* where
 16 a credit to the rich discipline of academic studies
 17 *graced* At Cambridge, an official 'grace' permits a candidate to proceed to his degree;
      Marlowe's name is entered in the Grace Book for 1584 and 1587

Excelling all, whose sweet delight disputes
In heavenly matters of theology.
Till, swollen with cunning, of a self conceit,   20
His waxen wings did mount above his reach,
And melting heavens conspired his overthrow.
For falling to a devilish exercise,
And glutted more with learning's golden gifts,
He surfeits upon cursed necromancy: 25
Nothing so sweet as magic is to him,
Which he prefers before his chiefest bliss.
And this the man that in his study sits.   *Exit*

Scene 1

Enter FAUSTUS *in his Study*

FAUSTUS
Settle thy studies, Faustus, and begin
To sound the depth of that thou wilt profess:
Having commenced, be a divine in show,
Yet level at the end of every art,
And live and die in Aristotle's works.   5
Sweet *Analytics*, 'tis thou hast ravished me:
Bene disserere est finis logices.

18 *whose sweet delight disputes* whose great pleasure is in academic debate
20 *cunning* knowledge; usually knowledge misapplied
    self conceit pride in his own abilities
21 *waxen wings* In Greek mythology, Icarus flew too near the sun on wings of wax; they
    melted, and he fell into the sea. The fall of Icarus became a popular Renaissance emblem
    throughout Europe
27 *chiefest bliss* i.e. hope of life after death
28 *this the man* This seems to be the cue for the Chorus to draw aside a curtain and disclose
    Faustus in his study

2 *sound* measure
   profess specialize in, study and teach
3 *commenced* graduated; a Cambridge term
   divine theologian
   in show in appearance
4 consider the purpose of every discipline
5–37 In his survey of human scholarship Faustus resembles the protagonist of Lyly's *Euphues*
      (1578) who determines to return to the university:

Is, to dispute well, logic's chiefest end?
Affords this art no greater miracle?
Then read no more, thou hast attained the end;   10
A greater subject fitteth Faustus' wit.
Bid *on kai me on* farewell; Galen come:
Seeing, *ubi desinit philosophus, ibi incipit medicus.*
Be a physician, Faustus, heap up gold,
And be eternized for some wondrous cure.   15
Summum bonum medicinae sanitas:
The end of physic is our body's health.
Why Faustus, hast thou not attained that end?
Is not thy common talk found aphorisms?
Are not thy bills hung up as monuments,   20

Philosophic, Phisicke, Divinitie, shal be my studie. O ye hidden secrets of Nature, the
expresse image of morall venues, the equall ballaunce of Justice, the medicines to heale
all diseases, how they beginne to delyght me. The *Axiomaes* of *Aristotle,* the *Maxims*
of *Justinian,* the *Aphorismes* of *Galen,* have sodaynelye made such a breache into my
minde, that I seem onely to desire them which did onely earst detest them.
                                        Euphues, ed. Bond (1902), i.241

5–7 Aristotle had been the dominant figure in the university curriculum since the thirteenth
century, but in Marlowe's day his supremacy was challenged by the intellectual reformer
Petrus Ramus. *Analytics* is the name given to two of Aristotle's works on the nature of proof
in argument, but the definition of logic in line 7 comes in fact from Ramus' *Dialecticae.*
Ramus, his ideas, and his violent death are displayed in Marlowe's *Massacre at Paris*

12 *on kai me on* being and not being. A1 prints a jumble of letters, 'Oncaymaeon', which
later editions, trying to make some sense out of them, changed to 'Oeconomy'. Bullen
recognized A's apparent gibberish as a transliteration of the Greek phrase, from a work
attributed to the philosopher Georgias of Leontini (*c.* 483–376 B.C.)
Galen A second-century Greek physician who was accepted as an authority on medical
science throughout the Middle Ages

13 since the doctor starts where the philosopher leaves off; Aristotle, *de sensu,* ch 1, 436a

14 *heap up gold* The association of gold and the medical profession is an old one; Shakespeare
mentions the use of gold for 'Preserving life in med'cine potable' (2 *Henry IV,* IV, v, 162).
Faustus, however, is thinking of the profit to be gained – like Chaucer's Physician in *The
Canterbury Tales:*

    For gold in phisik is a cordial,
    Therefore he lovede gold in special.   (Prologue, 444–5)

15 *eternized* immortalized

16 Aristotle, *Nicomachean Ethics,* 1094. a. 8; Faustus translates in line 17

19 Faustus ranks himself with Hippocrates, whose *Aphorismes* was the most famous of
medical textbooks
found B (sound A) thought to be

20 *bills* prescriptions

Whereby whole cities have escaped the plague,
And thousand desperate maladies been eased?
Yet art thou still but Faustus, and a man.
Couldst thou make men to live eternally,
Or, being dead, raise them to life again,   25
Then this profession were to be esteemed.
Physic farewell! Where is Justinian?
Si una eademque res legatur duobus,
Alter rem alter valorem rei, etc.
A pretty case of paltry legacies: 30
Exhereditare filium non potest pater nisi . . .
Such is the subject of the Institute,
And universal body of the law:
This study fits a mercenary drudge
Who aims at nothing but external trash!   35
Too servile and illiberal for me.
When all is done, divinity is best:
Jerome's Bible, Faustus, view it well:
Stipendium peccati mors est: ha! *Stipendium, etc.*
The reward of sin is death? That's hard.   40
Si peccasse negamus, fallimur, et nulla est in nobis veritas

---

21 *Whereby* i.e. through the efficacy of the drugs
24 *Could'st . . . men* B (Would'st . . . man A); B's emendation is justifiable on grounds of
    common sense: Faustus longs for the divine power to grant eternal life, or the power of
    Christ (who raised Lazarus from the dead: St John ii. 1–44)
27 Justinian was a Roman emperor of the sixth century A.D., who re-organized the whole
    of Roman Law in his *Corpus Juris* ('Body of the Law'); the first part, *Institutions*, was a
    manual intended for law-students
28–9 'If one and the same thing is bequeathed to two persons, one should have the thing itself,
    the other the value of the thing': Justinian, *Institutes*, ii. 20
31 'A father cannot disinherit his son unless . . .': Justinian, ii. 13
33 *law* B (church A)
34 *This study* B (His study A)
36 *Too servile* B (The devil A)
    illiberal Faustus compares the mercenary concerns of the lawyers with the culturally
    enriching studies of the 'liberal arts'
38 *Jerome's Bible* the Vulgate, prepared mainly by St Jerome; but the texts that Faustus quotes
    are not in the Latin of the Vulgate
39 Romans vi, 23; but Faustus reads only half of the verse
41 I John i, 8. By again reading only half the verse, Faustus fails to register the offered comfort:
    'If we confess our sins, he is faithful and just to forgive us our sins, and to cleanse us
    from all unrighteousness'

If we say that we have no sin,
We deceive ourselves, and there's no truth in us.
Why then belike we must sin,
And so consequently die. 45
Ay, we must die an everlasting death.
What doctrine call you this? *Che sara, sara*:
What will be, shall be! Divinity, adieu!
These metaphysics of magicians,
And necromantic books are heavenly! 50
Lines, circles, schemes, letters and characters!
Ay, these are those that Faustus most desires.
O what a world of profit and delight,
Of power, of honour, of omnipotence
Is promised to the studious artisan! 55
All things that move between the quiet poles
Shall be at my command: emperors and kings
Are but obeyed in their several provinces,
Nor can they raise the wind, or rend the clouds;
But his dominion that exceeds in this 60
Stretcheth as far as doth the mind of man:
A sound magician is a mighty god.
Here Faustus, try thy brains to gain a deity.

Enter WAGNER

Wagner, commend me to my dearest friends,
The German Valdes, and Cornelius, 65
Request them earnestly to visit me.
WAGNER
I will sir.   *Exit*
FAUSTUS
Their conference will be a greater help to me,
Than all my labours, plod I ne'er so fast.

---

48   'What will be, shall be'
51   *schemes* Gill (scenes A; *om* B); diagrams
55   *artisan* craftsman
56   *quiet poles* the poles of the universe, quiet because unmoving
58   *several* respective
60   *exceeds* excels
      this i.e. this magic art

Enter the GOOD ANGEL *and the* EVIL ANGEL

GOOD ANGEL
O Faustus, lay that damned book aside,   70
And gaze not on it, lest it tempt thy soul,
And heap God's heavy wrath upon thy head:
Read, read the Scriptures; that is blasphemy.

EVIL ANGEL
Go forward, Faustus, in that famous art,
Wherein all nature's treasury is contained: 75
Be thou on earth as Jove is in the sky,
Lord and commander of these elements.   *Exeunt*

FAUSTUS
How am I glutted with conceit of this!
Shall I make spirits fetch me what I please,
Resolve me of all ambiguities,   80
Perform what desperate enterprise I will?
I'll have them fly to India for gold,
Ransack the ocean for orient pearl,
And search all corners of the new found world
For pleasant fruits and princely delicates.   85
I'll have them read me strange philosophy,
And tell the secrets of all foreign kings;
I'll have them wall all Germany with brass,
And make swift Rhine circle fair Wittenberg;
I'll have them fill the public schools with silk,   90

---

76 *Jove* The names of the pagan deities were frequently attributed to the Christian God; there is special force in this coming from the Evil Angel
77 *these elements* the four elements – earth, air, fire, and water – of which the world was made
78 *glutted with conceit* drunk with the thought
80 *Resolve me of* give me the answers to
   ambiguities problems
81 *desperate* daring
83 *orient pearl* The most precious pearls were from the Indian Ocean
84 *new found* newly discovered
85 *delicates* delicacies
86 *read me* teach me
88 *wall . . . brass* Friar Bacon, in Greene's *Friar Bacon and Friar Bungay* (before 1592) intended to 'circle England round with brass' (ii. 29) when his magic schemes reached fruition
89 *swift Rhine* Wittenberg in fact stands on the river Elbe
90 *public schools* university lecturerooms
   silk Dyce (skill Qq (all quartos)); in Marlowe's day, undergraduates were ordered to dress soberly

Wherewith the students shall be bravely clad.
I'll levy soldiers with the coin they bring,
And chase the Prince of Parma from our land,
And reign sole king of all our provinces.
Yea, stranger engines for the brunt of war,   95
Than was the fiery keel at Antwerp's bridge,
I'll make my servile spirits to invent.
Come German Valdes and Cornelius,
And make me blest with your sage conference.

Enter VALDES *and* CORNELIUS

Valdes, sweet Valdes, and Cornelius,   100
Know that your words have won me at the last
To practise magic and concealed arts;
Yet not your words only, but mine own fantasy,
That will receive no object for my head,
But ruminates on necromantic skill.   105
Philosophy is odious and obscure,
Both law and physic are for petty wits;
Divinity is basest of the three,
Unpleasant, harsh, contemptible and vile.
'Tis magic, magic that hath ravished me.   110
Then, gentle friends, aid me in this attempt,
And I, that have with concise syllogisms
Gravelled the pastors of the German church,
And made the flowering pride of Wittenberg
Swarm to my problems, as the infernal spirits   115
On sweet Musaeus when he came to hell,

 91 *bravely* smartly
93–6 The Prince of Parma was Spanish governor-general of the United Provinces of the
      Netherlands, 1579–92; he had earlier been responsible for building a bridge across the Scheldt
      (in the blockade of Antwerp), which was attacked and destroyed by a fire-ship in April 1589
 95 *engines* machines
      brunt assault
102 *concealed* occult
103 *fantasy* imagination
104 'Which won't let me think of anything else'
112 *concise syllogisms* clever arguments
113 *Gravelled* confounded
115 *problems* topics of academic debate
116 *Musaeus* Virgil (*Aeneid* vi, 667–8) describes this legendary, pre-Homeric bard (*not* the
      author of *Hero and Leander*) surrounded by the spirits of priests and bards in the Elysian
      fields of the Greek underworld

Will be as cunning as Agrippa was,
Whose shadows made all Europe honour him.
VALDES
Faustus, these books, thy wit, and our experience
Shall make all nations to canonize us.　　　　120
As Indian Moors obey their Spanish lords,
So shall the spirits of every element
Be always serviceable to us three.
Like lions shall they guard us when we please,
Like Almaine rutters with their horsemen's staves,　　　125
Or Lapland giants trotting by our sides;
Sometimes like women, or unwedded maids,
Shadowing more beauty in their airy brows
Than in the white breasts of the Queen of Love.
From Venice shall they drag huge argosies,　　　130
And from America the golden fleece
That yearly stuffs old Philip's treasury,
If learned Faustus will be resolute.
FAUSTUS
Valdes, as resolute am I in this
As thou to live, therefore object it not.　　　135
CORNELIUS
The miracles that magic will perform
Will make thee vow to study nothing else.
He that is grounded in astrology,

117　*Agrippa* The magician and necromancer Henry Cornelius Agrippa von Nettesheim (1486–1535) was famous for his reputed power of invoking shades of the dead
121　*Indian Moors* American Indians
122　*spirits* B (subjects A); A's reading seems to be a mistaken attempt by the compositor to carry on the sense of the preceding line; the 'spirits' are the elemental genii
125　'Like German cavalry with lances'
126　*Lapland giants* On another occasion Marlowe refers to the inhabitants of the polar regions in this way: 'tall and sturdy men, Giants as big as hugy Polypheme' (2 *Tamburlaine*, I,i, 37–8)
129　*in the* Greg (in their A; has the B)
130　*From* A2 (For A1)
　　　argosies treasureships
131–2　America, whose richness is compared to the golden fleece sought by Jason and the Argonauts, paid annual tribute to Philip of Spain; 'stuffs' became 'stuffed' in the B Text, in recognition of the death of Philip II
135　*object it not* don't raise any objections
138　*grounded* well schooled

Enriched with tongues, well seen in minerals,
Hath all the principles magic doth require: 140
Then doubt not, Faustus, but to be renowned
And more frequented for this mystery,
Than heretofore the Delphian oracle.
The spirits tell me they can dry the sea,
And fetch the treasure of all foreign wrecks,   145
Ay, all the wealth that our forefathers hid
Within the massy entrails of the earth.
Then tell me, Faustus, what shall we three want?

FAUSTUS

Nothing Cornelius! O this cheers my soul!
Come, show me some demonstrations magical,   150
That I may conjure in some lusty grove,
And have these joys in full possession.

VALDES

Then haste thee to some solitary grove,
And bear wise Bacon's and Abanus' works,
The Hebrew Psalter, and New Testament;   155
And whatsoever else is requisite
We will inform thee ere our conference cease.

CORNELIUS

Valdes, first let him know the words of art,
And then, all other ceremonies learned,
Faustus may try his cunning by himself.   160

VALDES

First, I'll instruct thee in the rudiments,

---

139 *tongues* Greek and Hebrew were desirable for those who would converse with spirits, but Latin
     was the recognized common language: 'Thou art a scholar: speak to it Horatio.' *Hamlet*, I,i, 42
     seen in minerals B (seen minerals A); knowledgeable about the properties of minerals
142 'More sought after for practising this art'
143 *Delphian oracle* the oracle of Apollo at Delphi
147 *massy* solid
151 *lusty* A1 (little A2,3; bushy B); in the sixteenth century, the word could mean 'pleasant'
154 *wise Bacon's and Abanus'* works Roger Bacon (?1214–94), protagonist of Greene's *Friar
     Bacon and Friar Bungay*, was an Oxford philosopher popularly supposed to have dabbled
     in black magic. Abanus is perhaps Pietro d'Abano (?1250–1316), Italian humanist and
     physician, who was also believed to have been a conjuror. As well as the works of these
     two, which would supply formulae for incantation, Faustus would need certain Psalms
     (especially 22 and 51) and the opening words of St John's Gospel for his conjuring
161 *rudiments* 'all that which is called vulgarly the vertue of worde, herbe, & stone: which is
     used by unlawful charmes, without natural causes . . . such kinde of charmes as commonlie
     daft wives use.' James I, *Daemonologie* (Edinburgh, 1597), p. 11

And then wilt thou be perfecter than I.
FAUSTUS
    Then come and dine with me, and after meat
    We'll canvass every quiddity thereof:
    For ere I sleep, I'll try what I can do.   165
    This night I'll conjure, though I die therefore.   *Exeunt*

Scene 2

Enter two SCHOLARS

1 SCHOLAR
    I wonder what's become of Faustus, that was wont to make our
    schools ring with *sic probo*.
2 SCHOLAR
    That shall we know; for see, here comes his boy.

Enter WAGNER

1 SCHOLAR
    How now sirra, where's thy master?
WAGNER
    God in heaven knows.   5
2 SCHOLAR
    Why, dost not thou know?
WAGNER
    Yes I know, but that follows not.
1 SCHOLAR
    Go to sirra, leave your jesting, and tell us where he is.
WAGNER
    That follows not necessary by force of argument, that you, being
    licentiates, should stand upon't; therefore acknowledge your error,   10
    and be attentive.

---

164 *canvass every quiddity* explore every detail; *quiddity* is a scholastic term denoting the
     essence of a thing, that which makes it what it is

2 *sic probo* thus I prove it: a term from scholastic disputation
10 *licentiates* graduates; holders of a degree permitting them to study for higher (master's
     or doctor's) degrees
     stand upon't understand

2 SCHOLAR

Why, didst thou not say thou knew'st?

WAGNER

Have you any witness on't?

1 SCHOLAR

Yes sirra, I heard you.

WAGNER

Ask my fellow if I be a thief.   15

2 SCHOLAR

Well, you will not tell us.

WAGNER

Yes sir, I will tell you; yet if you were not dunces you
would never ask me such a question. For is not he *corpus
naturale*? And is not that *mobile*? Then wherefore should
you ask me such a question? But that I am by nature   20
phlegmatic, slow to wrath, and prone to lechery – to love I
would say – it were not for you to come within forty foot of
the place of execution, although I do not doubt to see you
both hanged the next sessions. Thus having triumphed over
you, I will set my countenance like a precisian, and begin to   25
speak thus: Truly my dear brethren, my master is within at
dinner with Valdes and Cornelius, as this wine, if it could
speak, it would inform your worships. And so the Lord
bless you, preserve you, and keep you, my dear brethren,
my dear brethren.   *Exit*   30

1 SCHOLAR

Nay then, I fear he is fallen into that damned art, for which
they two are infamous through the world.

12–15 This seems to have been the formula for some kind of stock theatrical 'business', drawing
       the audience into the comedy routine
    17 *dunces* blockheads. The followers of Duns Scotus were commonly known as Dunses,
       but here it is Wagner himself who indulges in the academic cavilling characteristic of
       the Scotists
18–19 *corpus . . . mobile* a natural body and [therefore] capable of movement: Aristotle's *corpus
       naturale seu mobile* was the current scholastic definition of the subject-matter of physics
    23 *place of execution* i.e. the dining-room; Wagner continues to make comic capital out of
       the phrase
    25 *precisian* puritan; Wagner now apes the unctuous speech of this sect

2 SCHOLAR

Were he a stranger, and not allied to me, yet should I grieve for
him. But come, let us go and inform the Rector, and see if he by
his grave counsel can reclaim him.   35

1 SCHOLAR

Ay, but I fear me nothing can reclaim him.

2 SCHOLAR

Yet let us try what we can do.   *Exeunt*

Scene 3

Enter FAUSTUS *to conjure*

FAUSTUS

Now that the gloomy shadow of the earth,
Longing to view Orion's drizzling look,
Leaps from th'antarctic world unto the sky,
And dims the welkin with her pitchy breath:
Faustus, begin thine incantations,   5
And try if devils will obey thy hest,
Seeing thou hast prayed and sacrificed to them.
Within this circle is Jehovah's name,
Forward and backward anagrammatized;
Th'abbreviated names of holy saints,   10
Figures of every adjunct to the heavens,

---

34 *Rector* head of the university

 1 *shadow of the earth* In *The French Academic*, La Primaudaye explains that 'the night, also,
    is no other thing than the shadow of the earth'. Cf. also John Norton Smith, 'Marlowe's
    Faustus', *N & Q* NS 25 (1978), pp. 436–7
 2 *Orion's drizzling look* the rainy constellation of Orion
 3 Marlowe seems to have thought that night advances from the southern hemisphere
 7 *prayed and sacrificed* A period of prayer and sacrifice, a kind of spiritual preparation,
    was a pre-requisite for conjuring
8–13 Before he began his conjuring, the magician would draw a circle round himself, inscribing
    on the periphery certain signs (of the zodiac, for instance) and the tetragrammaton, the
    four Hebrew letters of the Divine Name. This was not only part of the invocation: so long
    as the circle was unbroken and the magician stayed inside it, no evil spirit could harm him
 9 *anagrammatized* B (and agramathist A)
10 *Th'abbreviated* B (The breviated A)
11 *adjunct* heavenly body joined to the firmament (see note on Scene 5, lines 211–19)

And characters of signs and erring stars,
By which the spirits are enforced to rise.
Then fear not Faustus, but be resolute,
And try the uttermost magic can perform.   15
Sint mihi dei acherontis propitii. Valeat numen triplex
Jehovae! Ignei, aerii, terreni, aquatici spiritus salvete!
Orientis princeps, Belzebub inferni ardentis monarcha, et
Demogorgon, propitiamus vos, ut appareat et surgat Meph-
astophilis. Quid tu moraris? Per Jehovam, Gehennam, et   20
consecratam aquam quam nunc spargo; signumque crucis
quod nunc facio; et per vota nostra, ipse nunc surgat nobis
dicatus Mephastophilis.

12 *characters* symbols
    signs i.e. of the zodiac
    erring stars planets
16–23 'May the gods of Acheron look favourably upon me. Away with the spirit of the three-
    fold Jehovah. Welcome, spirits of fire, air, water, and earth. We ask your favour, O Prince
    of the East, Belzebub, the monarch of burning hell, and Demogorgon, that Mephastophilis
    may appear and rise. Why do you delay? By Jehovah, Gehenna, and the holy water which
    I now sprinkle, and the sign of the cross which I now form, and by our vows, may
    Mephastophilis himself now rise, compelled to obey us.'
        Rejecting the God of Heaven, the Christian God in Three Persons, Faustus turns to
    His infernal counterpart: Acheron is one of the rivers in the Greek underworld, the Prince
    of the East is Lucifer (see Isaiah xiv, 12), and Demogorgon is, in classical mythology, one
    of the most terrible primeval gods. Faustus hails the spirits of the elements: 'they make
    them believe, that at the fall of *Lucifer*, some spirits fell in the aire, some in the fire, some
    in the water, some in the lande' (*Daemonologie*, p. 20). The name of Mephastophilis was
    not, apparently, known before the Faust legend; this seems to have been Marlowe's
    preferred spelling – it is the one used most frequently in the A Text. The different spellings
    are discussed by William Empson in *Faustus and the Censor*, 1987.
        Many invocations to the devil express similar surprise and impatience at his delay,
    after which the conjuror redoubles his efforts. Gehenna, the valley of Hinnom, was a
    place of sacrifice. Dr Faustus seems now to be renouncing his Christian baptism, misusing
    the baptismal water and forswearing the vows made at his christening. In devil-worship,
    the sign of the cross had a double function: a powerful charm to overcome diabolic
    disobedience, it also protected the conjuror from injury by any spirit that might appear
17 *terreni* Greg (*om* Qq); Faustus would invoke the spirits of all four elements
18 *Belzebub* Marlowe's form of the name has been retained because at certain points (e.g. Scene
    5, line 12) this suits better with the metre than the more commonly used Hebraic Beelzebub
20 *Quid tu moraris* Ellis (*quod tumeraris* Qq)

Enter a DEVIL

I charge thee to return and change thy shape,
Thou art too ugly to attend on me;   25
Go and return an old Franciscan friar,
That holy shape becomes a devil best.   *Exit* DEVIL
I see there's virtue in my heavenly words!
Who would not be proficient in this art?
How pliant is this Mephastophilis,   30
Full of obedience and humility,
Such is the force of magic and my spells.
Now Faustus, thou art conjuror laureate
That canst command great Mephastophilis.
Quin redis, Mephastophilis, fratris imagine!   35

Enter MEPHASTOPHILIS

MEPHASTOPHILIS
Now Faustus, what would'st thou have me do?
FAUSTUS
I charge thee wait upon me whilst I live,
To do what ever Faustus shall command,
Be it to make the moon drop from her sphere,
Or the ocean to overwhelm the world.   40
MEPHASTOPHILIS
I am a servant to great Lucifer,
And may not follow thee without his leave;
No more than he commands must we perform.
FAUSTUS
Did not he charge thee to appear to me?
MEPHASTOPHILIS
No, I came now hither of mine own accord.   45

---

24 *change thy shape EFB* describes a creature of fire, which appears at this point and eventually
takes the shape of a man; the B Text asks for a 'Dragon' in what seems to be an anticipatory
stage direction, and the woodcut on the B titlepage shows an emergent dragon on the ground
beside the conjuror's circle. A wary magician always stipulated from the beginning that a
pleasing shape should be assumed
33 *laureate* The laurel wreath of excellence was given to poets in ancient Greece
35 'Why do you not return, Mephastophilis, in the likeness of a friar'
redis Boas (*regis* A; this line, and the two preceding ones, are omitted in B)
39–40 Faustus would share these powers with the enchanters of classical literature (see Kocher, p. 141)
45 What Kocher (p. 160) calls the 'doctrine of voluntary ascent' is fairly well established in witchcraft

FAUSTUS

Did not my conjuring speeches raise thee? Speak!

MEPHASTOPHILIS

That was the cause, but yet *per accidens*,
For when we hear one rack the name of God,
Abjure the Scriptures, and his saviour Christ,
We fly in hope to get his glorious soul,   50
Nor will we come, unless he use such means
Whereby he is in danger to be damned:
Therefore the shortest cut for conjuring
Is stoutly to abjure the Trinity,
And pray devoutly to the prince of hell.   55

FAUSTUS

So Faustus hath already done, and holds this principle:
There is no chief but only Belzebub,
To whom Faustus doth dedicate himself.
This word damnation terrifies not him,
For he confounds hell in Elysium: 60
His ghost be with the old philosophers.
But leaving these vain trifles of men's souls,
Tell me, what is that Lucifer thy lord?

MEPHASTOPHIUS

Arch-regent and commander of all spirits.

FAUSTUS

Was not that Lucifer an angel once?   65

MEPHASTOPHILIS

Yes Faustus, and most dearly loved of God.

FAUSTUS

How comes it then that he is prince of devils?

MEPHASTOPHILIS

O, by aspiring pride and insolence,

---

47 *per accidens* only in appearance; what the conjuring represented was the real cause
48 *rack* violate: 'take the name of the Lord in vain'
60 *confounds hell in Elysium* makes no distinction between the Christian concept of hell and the pagan (Greek) notion of the after-life in Elysium. Marlowe has already coupled the two: 'Hell and Elysium swarm with ghosts of men' (*1 Tamburlaine*, V,ii, 403). Nashe may be referring to either of these passages when he scorns the writers that 'thrust Elisium into hell' (Preface to Greene's *Menaphon* [1589], ed. McKerrow, iii, 316)
61 *old philosophers* those who shared his disbelief in an eternity of punishment; the line seems to come from a saying of Averroes: *sit anima mea cum philosophis* (cf. J. C. Maxwell, *N & Q*, CXIV [1949], pp. 334–5; J. M. Steadman, *N & Q*, CCVII [1962], pp. 327–9)
63 *that Lucifer* A simple account of the history of Lucifer is given in Isaiah xiv, 12–15

For which God threw him from the face of heaven.

FAUSTUS

And what are you that live with Lucifer?   70

MEPHASTOPHILIS

Unhappy spirits that fell with Lucifer,
Conspired against our God with Lucifer,
And are for ever damned with Lucifer.

FAUSTUS

Where are you damned?

MEPHASTOPHILIS

In hell.   75

FAUSTUS

How comes it then that thou art out of hell?

MEPHASTOPHILIS

Why this is hell, nor am I out of it.
Think'st thou that I, who saw the face of God,
And tasted the eternal joys of heaven,
Am not tormented with ten thousand hells   80
In being deprived of everlasting bliss!
O Faustus, leave these frivolous demands,
Which strike a terror to my fainting soul.

FAUSTUS

What, is great Mephastophilis so passionate
For being deprived of the joys of heaven?   85
Learn thou of Faustus manly fortitude,
And scorn those joys thou never shalt possess.
Go bear these tidings to great Lucifer,
Seeing Faustus hath incurred eternal death
By desperate thoughts against Jove's deity: 90

77–81 Caxton, while locating hell 'in the most lowest place, most derke, and most vyle of the
erthe', stressed that it is a state as well as a place; the condemned sinner is like a man 'that
had a grete maladye, so moche that he sholde deye, and that he were brought into a fair
place and plesaunt for to have Joye and solace; of so moche shold he be more hevy and
sorowful' (*The Mirrour of the World* [1480], ii, 18). Marlowe's concept of hell at this point
may be compared with Milton's; like Mephastophilis, Satan cannot escape:
> For within him Hell
> He brings, and round about him, nor from Hell
> One step, no more than from himself can fly
> By change of place.   *Paradise Lost*, iv, 20–23

Mephastophilis' account of the torment of deprivation is translated from St John
Chrysostom: *si decem mille gehennas quis dixerit, nihil tale est quale ab illa beata visione
excidere* (see John Searle, *T.L.S.*, 15 February 1936)

88 *these* B (*those* A)

[41]

Say, he surrenders up to him his soul
So he will spare him four and twenty years,
Letting him live in all voluptuousness,
Having thee ever to attend on me,
To give me whatsoever I shall ask, 95
To tell me whatsoever I demand,
To slay mine enemies, and aid my friends,
And always be obedient to my will.
Go, and return to mighty Lucifer,
And meet me in my study at midnight, 100
And then resolve me of thy master's mind.

MEPHASTOPHILIS
I will Faustus. *Exit*

FAUSTUS
Had I as many souls as there be stars
I'd give them all for Mephastophilis.
By him I'll be great emperor of the world, 105
And make a bridge through the moving air
To pass the ocean with a band of men;
I'll join the hills that bind the Afric shore,
And make that land continent to Spain,
And both contributory to my crown. 110
The emperor shall not live but by my leave,
Nor any potentate of Germany.
Now that I have obtained what I desire
I'll live in speculation of this art
Till Mephastophilis return again. *Exit* 115

Scene 4

Enter WAGNER *and the* CLOWN

WAGNER
Sirra boy, come hither.

92 *So* on condition that
106–7 Faustus plans to emulate Xerxes, who built a bridge (using boats) across the Hellespont
for his army to march over
108–9 The hills on either side of the Straits of Gibraltar would, if joined together, unite Africa
and Europe into a single continent

Scene 4 The B Text version of this scene, which is greatly changed to accommodate different
comedians and an altered theatrical taste, is printed in the Appendix

CLOWN

How, boy? Zounds, boy! I hope you have seen many boys
with such pickadevants as I have. Boy, quotha!

WAGNER

Tell me sirra, hast thou any comings in?

CLOWN

Ay, and goings out too; you may see else.   5

WAGNER

Alas poor slave, see how poverty jesteth in his nakedness!
The villain is bare, and out of service, and so hungry, that I
know he would give his soul to the devil for a shoulder of
mutton, though it were blood raw.

CLOWN

How, my soul to the devil for a shoulder of mutton though   10
'twere blood raw? Not so good friend; by'rlady, I had need
have it well roasted, and good sauce to it, if I pay so dear.

WAGNER

Well, wilt thou serve me, and I'll make thee go like *qui mihi
discipulus*?

CLOWN

How, in verse?   15

WAGNER

No sirra; in beaten silk and stavesacre.

CLOWN

How, how, knavesacre? Ay, I thought that was all the land
his father left him! Do ye hear, I would be sorry to rob you
of your living.

WAGNER

Sirra, I say in stavesacre.   20

---

3 *pickadevants* small, pointed beards
4 *comings in* earnings, income
5 *goings out* expenses; but the Clown makes the word serve two purposes, pointing also to
   his tattered clothing
7 *out of service* out of a job
13–14 *qui mihi discipulus* you who are my pupil: the opening words of a didactic Latin poem by
   the schoolmaster William Lily which would be familiar to every Elizabethan schoolboy
16 *beaten silk and stavesacre* 'In effect Wagner promises to dress his servant (or rather to
   dress him down) in silk – and adds that plenty of Keating's powder will be needed' (Greg).
   Gold or silver was hammered into silk as a kind of embroidery; *stavesacre* was a
   preparation from delphinium seeds used for killing fleas
17 *knavesacre* The Clown is fond of this kind of word-play, which was outdated by the
   time of Shakespeare's *Two Gentlemen of Verona* (*c*. 1594–5) where Speed shows a
   weary tolerance of Launce's jesting: 'Well, your old vice still: mistake the word' (III.i, 285)

CLOWN

Oho, oho, stavesacre! Why then belike, if I were your man,
I should be full of vermin.

WAGNER

So thou shalt, whether thou be'st with me or no. But sirra,
leave your jesting, and bind your self presently unto me for
seven years, or I'll turn all the lice about thee into familiars,   25
and they shall tear thee in pieces.

CLOWN

Do you hear sir? You may save that labour: they are too
familiar with me already – zounds, they are as bold with my
flesh as if they had paid for my meat and drink.

WAGNER

Well, do you hear sirra? Hold, take these guilders.   30

CLOWN

Gridirons; what be they?

WAGNER

Why, French crowns.

CLOWN

'Mass, but for the name of French crowns a man were as good
have as many English counters! And what should I do with these?

WAGNER

Why, now, sirra, thou art at an hour's warning whensoever   35
or wheresoever the devil shall fetch thee.

CLOWN

No, no, here take your gridirons again.

WAGNER

Truly I'll none of them.

32 French crowns, legal tender in England in the 16th and early 17th centuries, were easily
    counterfeited. Marlowe himself is reported in the Baines libel as having boasted 'That
    he had as good Right to Coine as the Queen of England and that . . . he ment, through
    the help of a Cunninge stamp maker to Coin ffrench Crownes pistoletes and English
    shillinges'. Among government measures to stop the flood of false coins was a proclamation
    of 1587 urging all who were offered such pieces to strike a hole in them (see Ruding,
    Annals of the Coinage of Britain [1817], i, 192ff); perhaps the Clown refers to such mutilation
    when he describes Wagner's coins as *gridirons*
33 '*Mass* by the holy mass
34 *counters* worthless tokens
38–42 The business with the coins must be similar to that in scene viii of *The Taming of A Shrew*
    where the Clown starts a sequence with 'Here, here, take your two shillings again'. The
    actors draw the audience into their comic play to 'Bear witness'

CLOWN

Truly but you shall.

WAGNER

Bear witness I gave them him.   40

CLOWN

Bear witness I give them you again.

WAGNER

Well, I will cause two devils presently to fetch thee away.
Baliol and Belcher!

CLOWN

Let your Baliol and your Belcher come here, and I'll knock
them, they were never so knocked since they were devils!   45
Say I should kill one of them, what would folks say? Do ye
see yonder tall fellow in the round slop, he has killed the
devil! So I should be called 'Killdevil' all the parish over.

> *Enter two* DEVILS, *and the* CLOWN *runs up*
> *and down crying*

WAGNER

Baliol and Belcher, spirits, away!   *Exeunt* [DEVILS]

CLOWN

What, are they gone? A vengeance on them! They have vile   50
long nails. There was a he devil and a she devil. I'll tell you how
you shall know them: all he devils has horns, and all she devils has
clefts and cloven feet.

WAGNER

Well sirra, follow me.

---

43 *Baliol* probably a corruption of 'Belial'; *Belcher* is also perhaps a mispronunciation of
'Belzebub'

44 *knock* beat

46–8 A similar passage occurs in *A Looking Glass for London* which was written by Lodge and
Greene, acted by Strange's Men in 1592, and printed in 1594. Here the Clown attacks the
devil who has come to carry him to hell; when the devil pleads that he is mortally
wounded, the Clown triumphs:

> Then may I count my selfe I thinke a tall man, that am able to kill a diuell. Now who
> dare deale with me in the parish, or what wench in *Ninivie* will not loue me, when
> they say, there goes he that beate the diuell.

(G3ᵛ)

47 *tall* fine
round slop baggy pants

53 *clefts* slits

CLOWN

But do you hear? If I should serve you, would you teach me   55
to raise up Banios and Belcheos?

WAGNER

I will teach thee to turn thy self to anything, to a dog, or a cat, or a
mouse, or a rat, or any thing.

CLOWN

How! A Christian fellow to a dog, or a cat, a mouse, or a
rat? No, no sir, if you turn me into anything, let it be in the   60
likeness of a little pretty frisking flea, that I may be here,
and there, and everywhere. O I'll tickle the pretty wenches'
plackets! I'll be amongst them i'faith.

WAGNER

Well sirra, come.

CLOWN

But, do you hear Wagner . . . ?   65

WAGNER

Baliol and Belcher!

CLOWN

O Lord I pray sir, let Banio and Belcher go sleep.

WAGNER

Villain, call me Master Wagner; and let thy left eye be
diametarily fixed upon my right heel, with *quasi vestigias
nostras insistere.*   *Exit*   70

CLOWN

God forgive me, he speaks Dutch fustian! Well, I'll follow
him, I'll serve him; that's flat.   *Exit*

---

61 *frisking flea* In the medieval 'Song of the Flea', the poet envies the flea because it has free
access to all parts of his mistress's body

69 *diametarily* diametrically

69–70 *quasi vestigias nostras insistere* as it were tread in our footsteps; the construction is false
(for *vestigiis nostris*), but this may be intentional

71 *Dutch fustian* gibberish – double Dutch; *fustian* is a coarse cloth made of flax and cotton

Scene 5

Enter FAUSTUS *in his Study*

FAUSTUS
   Now Faustus, must thou needs be damned,
   And canst thou not be saved.
   What boots it then to think of God or heaven?
   Away with such vain fancies and despair,
   Despair in God, and trust in Belzebub.   5
   Now go not backward: no, Faustus, be resolute;
   Why waverest thou? O, something soundeth in mine ears:
   'Abjure this magic, turn to God again'.
   Ay, and Faustus will turn to God again.
   To God? He loves thee not: 10
   The god thou servest is thine own appetite
   Wherein is fixed the love of Belzebub.
   To him I'll build an altar and a church,
   And offer luke-warm blood of new-born babes.

Enter GOOD ANGEL *and* EVIL [ANGEL]

GOOD ANGEL
   Sweet Faustus, leave that execrable art.   15
FAUSTUS
   Contrition, prayer, repentance: what of them?
GOOD ANGEL
   O they are means to bring thee unto heaven.
EVIL ANGEL
   Rather illusions, fruits of lunacy,
   That makes men foolish that do trust them most.
GOOD ANGEL
   Sweet Faustus, think of heaven, and heavenly things.   20
EVIL ANGEL
   No Faustus, think of honour and of wealth.
                    Exeunt [ANGELS]
FAUSTUS
   Of wealth!

21 *and of wealth* A2 (and wealth A1)

[47]

Why, the signory of Emden shall be mine
When Mephastophilis shall stand by me.
What god can hurt thee, Faustus? Thou art safe,   25
Cast no more doubts. Come Mephastophilis,
And bring glad tidings from great Lucifer.
Is't not midnight? Come Mephastophilis:
Veni veni Mephastophile.

Enter MEPHASTOPHILIS

Now tell me, what says Lucifer thy lord?   30
MEPHASTOPHILIS
That I shall wait on Faustus whilst he lives,
So he will buy my service with his soul.
FAUSTUS
Already Faustus hath hazarded that for thee.
MEPHASTOPHILIS
But Faustus, thou must bequeath it solemnly,
And write a deed of gift with thine own blood,   35
For that security craves great Lucifer.
If thou deny it, I will back to hell.
FAUSTUS
Stay Mephastophilis, and tell me,
What good will my soul do thy lord?
MEPHASTOPHILIS
Enlarge his kingdom.   40
FAUSTUS
Is that the reason he tempts us thus?
MEPHASTOPHILIS
Solamen miseris socios habuisse doloris.

---

23 *signory of Emden* governorship of Emden – a port on the mouth of the Ems, at this time
    trading extensively with England
29 'Come, O come Mephastophilis'
30 *tell me what* B (tell what A)
31 *the lives* B (I live A)
32 *So* provided that
33 *hazarded* jeopardized
40 *Enlarge to kingdom* 'Satan's chiefest drift & main point that he aimeth at, is the inlargement
    of his own kingdom, by the eternall destruction of man in the life to come', James Mason,
    The Anatomie of Sorcerie (1612), p. 55
42 In Chaucer's version: 'Men seyn, "to wrecche is consolacioun To have an-other felawe in
    his peyne".' *Troilus and Criseyde*, i, 708–9

FAUSTUS
  Have you any pain that torture others?
MEPHASTOPHILIS
  As great as have the human souls of men.
  But tell me Faustus, shall I have thy soul?   45
  And I will be thy slave and wait on thee,
  And give thee more than thou hast wit to ask.
FAUSTUS
  Ay Mephastophilis, I give it thee.
MEPHASTOPHILIS
  Then stab thine arm courageously,
  And bind thy soul, that at some certain day   50
  Great Lucifer may claim it as his own,
  And then be thou as great as Lucifer.
FAUSTUS
  Lo Mephastophilis, for love of thee,
  I cut mine arm, and with my proper blood
  Assure my soul to be great Lucifer's,   55
  Chief lord and regent of perpetual night.
  View here the blood that trickles from mine arm,
  And let it be propitious for my wish.
MEPHASTOPHILIS
  But Faustus, thou must write it
  In manner of a deed of gift.   60
FAUSTUS
  Ay, so I will; but Mephastophilis,
  My blood congeals and I can write no more.
MEPHASTOPHILIS
  I'll fetch thee fire to dissolve it straight.   *Exit*
FAUSTUS
  What might the staying of my blood portend?
  Is it unwilling I should write this bill?   65
  Why streams it not, that I may write afresh:
  'Faustus gives to thee his soul': ah, there it stayed!

43 *torture* B (tortures A)
54 *proper* own
58 *propitious* an acceptable sacrifice – as the blood of Christ is a propitiation for the sins of
     mankind

Why should'st thou not? Is not thy soul thine own?
Then write again: 'Faustus gives to thee his soul'.

Enter MEPHASTOPHILIS *with a chafer of coals*

MEPHASTOPHILIS
Here's fire, come Faustus, set it on.   70
FAUSTUS
So, now the blood begins to clear again.
Now will I make an end immediately.
MEPHASTOPHILIS
O what will not I do to obtain his soul!
FAUSTUS
Consummatum est, this bill is ended,
And Faustus hath bequeathed his soul to Lucifer.   75
But what is this inscription on mine arm?
Homo fuge. Whither should I fly?
If unto God, he'll throw thee down to hell;
My senses are deceived, here's nothing writ;
I see it plain, here in this place is writ,   80
Homo fuge! Yet shall not Faustus fly.
MEPHASTOPHILIS
I'll fetch him somewhat to delight his mind.   *Exit*

Enter [again] with DEVILS, *giving crowns and rich
apparel to* FAUSTUS; *they dance, and then depart*

FAUSTUS
Speak Mephastophilis, what means this show?
MEPHASTOPHILIS
Nothing Faustus, but to delight thy mind withal,
And to show thee what magic can perform.   85
FAUSTUS
But may I raise up spirits when I please?
MEPHASTOPHILIS
Ay Faustus, and do greater things than these.

---

69 s.d. *chafer* portable grate
70 *set it on* 'set his blood in a saucer on warm ashes' *EFB*, vi
71 Greg observes that no earthly fire will liquefy congealed blood
74 *Consummatum est* It is completed; the last words of Christ on the cross: St John xix, 30
77 *Homo fuge* Fly, O man

FAUSTUS
  Then there's enough for a thousand souls!
  Here Mephastophilis, receive this scroll,
  A deed of gift of body and of soul: 90
  But yet conditionally, that thou perform
  All articles prescribed between us both.
MEPHASTOPHILIS
  Faustus, I swear by hell and Lucifer
  To effect all promises between us made.
FAUSTUS
  Then hear me read them. On these conditions following: 95
  First, that Faustus may be a spirit in form and substance.
  Secondly, that Mephastophilis shall be his servant, and at
  his command.
  Thirdly, that Mephastophilis shall do for him, and bring him
  whatsoever.   100
  Fourthly, that he shall be in his chamber or house invisible.
  Lastly, that he shall appear to the said John Faustus at all
  times, in what form or shape soever he please.
  I, John Faustus of Wittenberg, doctor, by these presents, do
  give both body and soul to Lucifer, Prince of the East, and   105
  his minister Mephastophilis; and furthermore grant unto
  them that, four and twenty years being expired, the articles
  above written inviolate, full power to fetch or carry the said
  John Faustus, body and soul, flesh, blood, or goods, into their
  habitation wheresoever.   110
                                          By me John Faustus.
MEPHASTOPHILIS
  Speak Faustus, do you deliver this as your deed?
FAUSTUS
  Ay, take it; and the devil give thee good on't.
MEPHASTOPHILIS
  Now Faustus, ask what thou wilt.
FAUSTUS
  First will I question with thee about hell: 115

---

96 *a spirit* A spirit, to the Elizabethans, was usually an evil one – a devil (see Shakespeare,
    Sonnet CXLIV); according to some theologians, who followed Aquinas, God could have
    no mercy on a devil who was *ipso facto* incapable of repenting. See lines 189–91
104 *these presents* the legal articles

Tell me, where is the place that men call hell?

MEPHASTOPHILIS

Under the heavens.

FAUSTUS

Ay, but whereabouts?

MEPHASTOPHILIS

Within the bowels of these elements,
Where we are tortured and remain for ever.   120
Hell hath no limits, nor is circumscribed
In one self place; for where we are is hell,
And where hell is, must we ever be.
And to conclude, when all the world dissolves,
And every creature shall be purified,   125
All places shall be hell that is not heaven.

FAUSTUS

Come, I think hell's a fable.

MEPHASTOPHILIS

Ay, think so still, till experience change thy mind.

FAUSTUS

Why? think'st thou then that Faustus shall be damned?

MEPHASTOPHILIS

Ay, of necessity, for here's the scroll   130
Wherein thou hast given thy soul to Lucifer.

FAUSTUS

Ay, and body too; but what of that?
Thinkest thou that Faustus is so fond to imagine
That after this life there is any pain?
Tush, these are trifles and mere old wives' tales.   135

MEPHASTOPHILIS

But Faustus, I am an instance to prove the contrary;
For I am damned, and am now in hell.

FAUSTUS

How, now in hell? Nay, and this be hell, I'll willingly be
damned here! What, walking, disputing, etc . . . But leaving
off this, let me have a wife, the fairest maid in Germany, for I   140

---

119 *these elements* the four elements (fire, air, earth, and water) below the sphere of the moon

122 *one self place* one particular place

133 *fond* foolish

138ff The writing here seems to degenerate as the text becomes merely an excuse for some stage business with the devil-wife

139 *disputing* According to the Prologue (line 18) this is Faustus's great delight

am wanton and lascivious, and cannot live without a wife.

MEPHASTOPHILIS

How, a wife? I prithee Faustus, talk not of a wife.

FAUSTUS

Nay sweet Mephastophilis, fetch me one, for I will have one.

MEPHASTOPHILIS

Well, thou wilt have one; sit there till I come.

I'll fetch thee a wife in the devil's name.   *Exit*   145

Enter [again] with a DEVIL *dressed like a woman,*
with fireworks

MEPHASTOPHILIS

Tell Faustus, how dost thou like thy wife?

FAUSTUS

A plague on her for a hot whore!

MEPHASTOPHILIS

Tut Faustus, marriage is but a ceremonial toy;
If thou lovest me, think no more of it.
I'll cull thee out the fairest courtesans,   150
And bring them every morning to thy bed:
She whom thine eye shall like, thy heart shall have,
Be she as chaste as was Penelope,
As wise as Saba, or as beautiful
As was bright Lucifer before his fall.   155
Hold, take this book, peruse it thoroughly:
The iterating of these lines brings gold;
The framing of this circle on the ground
Brings whirlwinds, tempests, thunder and lightning.
Pronounce this thrice devoutly to thy self,   160
And men in armour shall appear to thee,
Ready to execute what thou desirest.

FAUSTUS

Thanks Mephastophilis, yet fain would I have a book
wherein I might behold all spells and incantations, that I
might raise up spirits when I please.   165

---

148 *ceremonial toy* trifling ceremony
149 *think no more* B (think more A)
150 *cull* pick
153 *Penelope* wife of Ulysses, renowned for her fidelity to an absent husband
154 *Saba* the Queen of Sheba, who confronted Solomon with 'hard questions', 1 Kings x

MEPHASTOPHILIS

   Here they are in this book.   *There turn to them*

FAUSTUS

   Now would I have a book where I might see all characters
   and planets of the heavens, that I might know their motions
   and dispositions.

MEPHASTOPHILIS

   Here they are too.   *Turn to them*   170

FAUSTUS

   Nay, let me have one book more, and then I have done,
   wherein I might see all plants, herbs and trees that grow
   upon the earth.

MEPHASTOPHILIS

   Here they be.

FAUSTUS

   O thou art deceived!   175

MEPHASTOPHILIS

   Tut, I warrant thee.   *Turn to them*

FAUSTUS

   When I behold the heavens, then I repent,
   And curse thee, wicked Mephastophilis,
   Because thou hast deprived me of those joys.

MEPHASTOPHILIS

   Why Faustus,   180
   Think'st thou that heaven is such a glorious thing?
   I tell thee 'tis not half so fair as thou,
   Or any man that breathes on earth.

FAUSTUS

   How prov'st thou that?

MEPHASTOPHILIS

   It was made for man, therefore is man more excellent.   185

FAUSTUS

   If it were made for man, 'twas made for me:
   I will renounce this magic, and repent.

               Enter GOOD ANGEL *and* EVIL ANGEL

GOOD ANGEL

   Faustus repent, yet God will pity thee.

EVIL ANGEL

   Thou art a spirit, God cannot pity thee.

FAUSTUS

Who buzzeth in mine ears I am a spirit?   190
Be I a devil, yet God may pity me.
Ay, God will pity me if I repent.

EVIL ANGEL

Ay, but Faustus never shall repent.

Exeunt [ANGELS]

FAUSTUS

My heart's so hardened I cannot repent!
Scarce can I name salvation, faith, or heaven,   195
But fearful echoes thunders in mine ears,
'Faustus, thou art damned'; then swords and knives,
Poison, guns, halters, and envenomed steel,
Are laid before me to dispatch myself:
And long ere this I should have slain myself,   200
Had not sweet pleasure conquered deep despair.
Have not I made blind Homer sing to me
Of Alexander's love, and Oenon's death?
And hath not he that built the walls of Thebes
With ravishing sound of his melodious harp,   205
Made music with my Mephastophilis?
Why should I die then, or basely despair?
I am resolved! Faustus shall ne'er repent.
Come Mephastophilis, let us dispute again,
And argue of divine astrology.   210

190   *buzzeth* whispers
191   *Be I* This could mean either 'Even if I am', or else 'Even though I were'
194   Hardness (also called blindness) of heart is recognized as a very complex spiritual
      condition; the Litany of the Book of Common Prayer offers a special supplication: 'From
      all blindness of heart . . . Good Lord, deliver us'
198   *halters* hangman's ropes
202   *blind Homer* The Greek poet was traditionally held to be blind
203   *Alexander . . . death* Alexander (Homer's name for Paris, son of Priam) fell in love with
      Oenone before he encountered Helen. After he was wounded in the Trojan War, he was
      carried to Oenone and died at her feet, whereupon she stabbed herself
204–5 At the sound of Amphion's harp the stones were so affected that they rose of their own
      accord to form the walls of Thebes
210–39 The Faustus of Marlowe's source was an astrologer – a calendar-maker and weather-
      forecaster – rather than an astronomer; and although the spirit promises to teach
      him about the planets, his approach is unscientific and the information a
      miscellaneous jumble. Marlowe's protagonist has the questioning mind of the

Tell me, are there many heavens above the moon?
Are all celestial bodies but one globe,
As is the substance of this centric earth?

MEPHASTOPHILIS

As are the elements, such are the spheres,
Mutually folded in each other's orb.   215
And, Faustus, all jointly move upon one axletree
Whose termine is termed the world's wide pole,
Nor are the names of Saturn, Mars, or Jupiter,
Feigned, but are erring stars.

FAUSTUS

But tell me, have they all one motion, both *situ et*   220
tempore?

Renaissance student, and the answers he is given accord with the sceptical authorities
of the day (see Kocher, pp. 214–23 and F. R. Johnson, 'Marlowe's Astronomy and
Renaissance Skepticism', *E.L.H.*, XIII [1946], iv). The Ptolemaic system, as yet unshaken
by Copernicus, held that the universe was composed of concentric spheres with the
earth (*this centric earth*) as the innermost. Beyond the earth was the sphere of the
Moon, and further out still the spheres of the six other *erring stars* or planets: Mercury,
Venus, Sun, Mars, Jupiter, Saturn. The eighth was the firmament, or sphere of the
fixed stars, which Marlowe, admitting only nine spheres (1. 235) identified with the
Primum Mobile, the first moving thing which imparted movement to all the rest. The
ninth sphere (tenth, if the *Primum Mobile* was allowed to be separate from the
firmament) was the immovable empyrean (*the empyreal orb*)

211–19   *Tell me . . . erring stars* Faustus asks first for confirmation of the number of spheres
beyond the Moon, and whether in fact these do form a single ball. Mephastophilis replies
that just as the four elements enclose each other (earth is surrounded by water, water by
air, and air by fire), so each sphere or heaven is circled round by the ones beyond it, and
all rotate upon a single axletree. Saturn, Mars, and the other planets are individually
recognizable: they are called *erring* or wandering stars to distinguish them from the fixed
stars which are joined to the firmament

217   *termine* boundary (astronomical)

220–31   *But . . . days* 'Do all the planets move at the same speed and in the same direction?'
is Faustus' next question. He is told that the planets have two movements: a daily west to
east rotation round the earth governed by the *Primum Mobile,* and a slower, individual
turning from west to east. Caxton (*Mirrour of the World* [1480], i, 13) explains that each
planet is like a fly crawling on a wheel: if the fly crawls in one direction and the wheel turns
in the opposite, the fly may be said to have two motions. Faustus knows this well enough,
and proceeds to detail with reasonable accuracy the different times taken by the planets in
their individual revolutions – the farthest from the earth, naturally, taking the longest. The
figures usually given are: Saturn 29½ years; Jupiter 11¾ years; Mars 1 year 11 months; Sun 1
year; Venus 7½ months; and Mercury 3 months

220–1   *situ et tempore* in direction and time

MEPHASTOPHILIS

All jointly move from east to west in four-and-twenty
hours upon the poles of the world, but differ in their
motion upon the poles of the zodiac.

FAUSTUS

Tush, these slender trifles Wagner can decide!   225
Hath Mephastophilis no greater skill?
Who knows not the double motion of the planets?
The first is finished in a natural day, the second thus: as
Saturn in thirty years; Jupiter in twelve; Mars in four; the
Sun, Venus, and Mercury in a year; the Moon in twenty-   230
eight days. Tush, these are freshmen's suppositions. But
tell me, hath every sphere a dominion or *intelligentia*?

MEPHASTOPHILIS

Ay.

FAUSTUS

How many heavens or spheres are there?

MEPHASTOPHILIS

Nine: the seven planets, the firmament, and the empyreal   235
heaven.

FAUSTUS

Well, resolve me in this question: why have we not

---

231 *freshmen's suppositions* elementary facts given to first-year undergraduates for them to
build an argument upon

232 *hath . . . intelligentia* The next question at issue relates to a theory first propounded by
Plato and developed in the Middle Ages, that each planet was guided by an angelic spirit,
commonly called the *intelligence*:

    Let mans Soule be a Spheare, and then, in this,
    The intelligence that moves, devotion is.
                    Donne, 'Good Friday, Riding Westwards'

Mephastophilis affirms the *intelligence*, but the theory was never really accepted by
scientists

234–6 *How many . . . heaven* Faustus seems to return to his earlier query about the number of
spheres or heavens. Aristotle accounted for eight, but another was added by the early
Church Fathers who postulated the *empyreal heaven* which was the abode of God,
unmoving and shining with a piercing, stainless light. Milton describes a similar cosmology
in *Paradise Lost* when he identifies 'the planets seven', 'the fixed', 'And that crystalline
sphere . . . that first moved' (III, 481–3)

237–40 *Resolve me . . . totius* Mephastophilis' answer to the next question sounds like a quot-
ation from some astronomical textbook. Faustus asks about the behaviour of the
planets, using technical but well-known astronomical terms; *conjunctions* are the apparent
joinings together of two planets, whilst *oppositions* describes their relationships when
most remote:

conjunctions, oppositions, aspects, eclipses, all at one time,
but in some years we have more, in some less?
MEPHASTOPHILIS
Per inaequalem motum respectu totius.   240
FAUSTUS
Well, I am answered. Tell me who made the world?
MEPHASTOPHILIS
I will not.
FAUSTUS
Sweet Mephastophilis, tell me.
MEPHASTOPHILIS
Move me not, for I will not tell thee.
FAUSTUS
Villain, have I not bound thee to tell me anything?   245
MEPHASTOPHILIS
Ay, that is not against our kingdom; but this is.
Think thou on hell Faustus, for thou art damned.
FAUSTUS
Think, Faustus, upon God, that made the world.
MEPHASTOPHILIS
Remember this.   *Exit*
FAUSTUS
Ay, go accursed spirit, to ugly hell,   250
'Tis thou hast damned distressed Faustus' soul:
Is't not too late?

Enter GOOD ANGEL *and* EVIL [ANGEL]

EVIL ANGEL
Too late.

Therefore the love which us doth bind,
But Fate so enviously debars,
Is the Conjunction of the Mind,
And Opposition of the Stars.

Marvell, 'The Definition of Love'

Any position between the two extremes of conjunction and opposition was termed an *aspect*. To astrologers the differing situations and relations of the planets all have some particular significance – hence the horoscope. Faustus is finally told what he already knows: that the heavenly bodies do not all move at the same speed, and that for this reason ('through an irregular motion so far as the whole is concerned', l. 240) there are more eclipses etc. in some years than in others

244 *Move me not* Don't make me angry

GOOD ANGEL
  Never too late, if Faustus can repent.
EVIL ANGEL
  If thou repent, devils shall tear thee in pieces.   255
GOOD ANGEL
  Repent, and they shall never rase thy skin.

                                        Exeunt [ANGELS]

FAUSTUS
  Ah Christ my Saviour, seek to save
  Distressed Faustus' soul.

         Enter LUCIFER, BELZEBUB *and* MEPHASTOPHILIS

LUCIFER
  Christ cannot save thy soul, for he is just.
  There's none but I have interest in the same.   260
FAUSTUS
  O who art thou that look'st so terrible?
LUCIFER
  I am Lucifer, and this is my companion prince in hell.
FAUSTUS
  O Faustus, they are come to fetch away thy soul!
LUCIFER
  We come to tell thee thou dost injure us.
  Thou talk'st of Christ, contrary to thy promise.   265
  Thou should'st not think of God; think of the devil,
  And of his dam too.
FAUSTUS
  Nor will I henceforth: pardon me in this,
  And Faustus vows never to look to heaven,
  Never to name God, or to pray to him,   270
  To burn his Scriptures, slay his ministers,
  And make my spirits pull his churches down.
LUCIFER
  Do so, and we will highly gratify thee. Faustus, we are
  come from hell to show thee some pastime; sit down, and
  thou shalt see all the Seven Deadly Sins appear in their   275
  proper shapes.

---

256 *rase* graze
260 *have interest in* have a legal claim on

[59]

FAUSTUS

That sight will be as pleasing unto me, as Paradise was to Adam, the first day of his creation,

LUCIFER

Talk not of Paradise, nor creation, but mark this show; talk of the devil and nothing else. Come away.   280

Enter the SEVEN DEADLY SINS

Now Faustus, examine them of their several names and dispositions.

FAUSTUS

What art thou, the first?

PRIDE

I am Pride: I disdain to have any parents. I am like to Ovid's flea, I can creep into every corner of a wench: 285
sometimes like a periwig, I sit upon her brow; or like a fan of feathers, I kiss her lips. Indeed I do – what do I not! But fie, what a scent is here? I'll not speak another word, except the ground were perfumed and covered with cloth of arras.

FAUSTUS

What are thou, the second?   290

COVETOUSNESS

I am Covetousness, begotten of an old churl in an old leathern bag: and might I have my wish, I would desire that this house, and all the people in it, were turned to gold, that I might lock you up in my good chest. O my sweet gold!

FAUSTUS

What art thou, the third?   295

WRATH

I am Wrath. I had neither father nor mother: I leaped out of a lion's mouth when I was scarce half an hour old, and ever since I have run up and down the world, with this case of rapiers, wounding myself when I had nobody to fight

---

281 *several* different
285 *Ovid's flea* The poet of 'Song of the Flea' (probably medieval but attributed to Ovid) envies the flea for its freedom of movement over his mistress' body
289 *cloth of arras* tapestry, woven at Arras in Flanders and used to make wall-hangings
292 *leathern bag* the miser's purse
298 *case* pair

withal. I was born in hell – and look to it, for some of you   300
shall be my father.

FAUSTUS

What art thou, the fourth?

ENVY

I am Envy, begotten of a chimney-sweeper, and an oyster-
wife. I cannot read, and therefore wish all books were
burnt; I am lean with seeing others eat – O that there   305
would come a famine through all the world, that all might
die, and I live alone; then thou should'st see how fat I
would be! But must thou sit and I stand? Come down, with
a vengeance.

FAUSTUS

Away, envious rascal! What art thou, the fifth?   310

GLUTTONY

Who, I sir? I am Gluttony. My parents are all dead, and the
devil a penny they have left me but a bare pension, and
that is thirty meals a day and ten bevers – a small trifle to
suffice nature. O, I come of a royal parentage: my
grandfather was a gammon of bacon, my grandmother a   315
hogshead of claret wine; my godfathers were these: Peter
Pickled-Herring, and Martin Martlemas-Beef. O, but my
godmother! She was a jolly gentlewoman, and well-beloved
in every good town and city; her name was Mistress
Margery March-Beer. Now, Faustus, thou hast heard all   320
my progeny; wilt thou bid me to supper?

FAUSTUS

Ho, I'll see thee hanged; thou wilt eat up all my victuals.

GLUTTONY

Then the devil choke thee!

FAUSTUS

Choke thyself, Glutton. What art thou, the sixth?

SLOTH

I am Sloth; I was begotten on a sunny bank, where I have   325

---

300 *some of you* Wrath addresses the audience
303–4 *begotten . . . wife* Envy is filthy, and stinks
313 *bevers* snacks
317 *Martlemas-Beef* Meat, salted to preserve it for winter, was hung up around Martinmas
(11 November)
320 *March-Beer* a rich ale, made in March and left to mature for at least two years
321 *progeny* lineage (obsolete)

lain ever since – and you have done me great injury to bring me from thence. Let me be carried thither again by Gluttony and Lechery. I'll not speak another word for a king's ransom.

FAUSTUS

What are you Mistress Minx, the seventh and last?   330

LECHERY

Who, I, sir? I am one that loves an inch of raw mutton better than an ell of fried stockfish; and the first letter of my name begins with Lechery.

LUCIFER

Away! To hell, to hell!

Exeunt the [SEVEN DEADLY] SINS

Now Faustus, how dost thou like this?   335

FAUSTUS

O this feeds my soul.

LUCIFER

Tut Faustus, in hell is all manner of delight.

FAUSTUS

O might I see hell, and return again, how happy were I then!

LUCIFER

Thou shalt; I will send for thee at midnight. In meantime,   340
take this book, peruse it thoroughly, and thou shalt turn thyself into what shape thou wilt.

FAUSTUS

Great thanks, mighty Lucifer; this will I keep as chary as my life.

LUCIFER

Farewell, Faustus; and think on the devil.   345

FAUSTUS

Farewell, great Lucifer; come Mephastophilis.

Exeunt omnes

331–3 *I am one ... Lechery* The words are rather obscure, but their sense is clear. Lechery prefers a small quantity of virility to a large extent of impotence: *stockfish*, a long strip of dried cod, is a common term of abuse, indicating impotence: 'he was begot between two stockfishes', *Measure for Measure*, III, ii, 98. The 'Minx' ends with a common form of jest: cf. 'Her name begins with Mistress Purge', Middleton, *The Family of Love*, II,iii, 53
343   *chary* carefully

Scene 6

Enter ROBIN *the ostler with a book in his hand*

ROBIN

O this is admirable! here I ha' stolen one of Doctor Faustus'
conjuring books, and i'faith I mean to search some circles
for my own use: now will I make all the maidens in our
parish dance at my pleasure stark naked before me, and so
by that means I shall see more than ere I felt, or saw yet.   5

Enter RAFE *calling* ROBIN

RAFE

Robin, prithee come away, there's a gentleman tarries to
have his horse, and he would have his things rubbed and
made clean. He keeps such a chafing with my mistress
about it, and she has sent me to look thee out. Prithee, come
away.   10

ROBIN

Keep out, keep out; or else you are blown up, you are
dismembered, Rafe. Keep out, for I am about a roaring
piece of work.

RAFE

Come, what dost thou with that same book? Thou canst not
read!   15

ROBIN

Yes, my master and mistress shall find that I can read – he for his
forehead, she for her private study. She's born to bear with me, or
else my art fails.

RAPE

Why Robin, what book is that?

ROBIN

What book? Why the most intolerable book for conjuring   20

Scene 6   In the A Text the two episodes with Robin and Rafe are presented as a single scene
     following Chorus 3 – which is surely intended to introduce the scene at the papal court.
     This edition follows the B Text in its division and placing of the episodes, but the content
     of the scenes is that of the A Text; the Appendix prints B's version

  2 *circles* magicians' circles; but the sexual overtones are obvious

  8 *chafing* scolding

  12 *roaring* dangerous

  20 *intolerable* Robin probably means 'incomparable'

that ere was invented by any brimstone devil.

RAFE

Canst thou conjure with it?

ROBIN

I can do all these things easily with it: first, I can make thee
drunk with 'ipocrase at any tavern in Europe for nothing,
that's one of my conjuring works.   25

RAFE

Our master parson says that's nothing.

ROBIN

True Rafe! And more, Rafe, if thou hast any mind to Nan Spit, our
kitchen-maid, then turn her and wind her to thy own use, as often
as thou wilt, and at midnight.

RAFE

O brave Robin! Shall I have Nan Spit, and to mine own   30
use? On that condition I'll feed thy devil with horsebread as
long as he lives, of free cost.

ROBIN

No more, sweet Rafe; let's go and make clean our boots
which lie foul upon our hands, and then to our conjuring
in the devil's name.   *Exeunt*   35

Chorus 2

Enter WAGNER *solus*

WAGNER

Learned Faustus,
To know the secrets of astronomy
Graven in the book of Jove's high firmament,
Did mount himself to scale Olympus' top,

---

24 *'ipocrase* hippocras – a spiced wine
31 *horsebread* fodder for horses
32 *of free cost* free of charge

1 s.d. *Enter Wagner* This direction from the A Text suggests that all the choric speeches –
   including the Prologue and the Epilogue – were spoken by Wagner
4 *Olympus* Mount Olympus was the home of the gods of Greek mythology

Being seated in a chariot burning bright, 5
Drawn by the strength of yoked dragons' necks.
He now is gone to prove cosmography,
And, as I guess, will first arrive at Rome,
To see the pope, and manner of his court,
And take some part of holy Peter's feast, 10
That to this day is highly solemnized. *Exit* WAGNER

Scene 7

Enter FAUSTUS *and* MEPHASTOPHILIS

FAUSTUS

Having now, my good Mephastophilis,
Passed with delight the stately town of Trier,
Environed round with airy mountain tops,
With walls of flint, and deep entrenched lakes,
Not to be won by any conquering prince; 5
From Paris next, coasting the realm of France,
We saw the river Main fall into Rhine,
Whose banks are set with groves of fruitful vines;
Then up to Naples, rich Campania,
Whose buildings fair and gorgeous to the eye, 10
The streets straight forth, and paved with finest brick,
Quarters the town in four equivalents;
There saw we learned Maro's golden tomb,
The way he cut, an English mile in length,
Thorough a rock of stone in one night's space. 15

---

6 *yoked* B (yoky A)
7 *cosmography* The B Text adds a line explaining that this 'measures costs, and kingdomes of the earth'
10 *holy Peter's feast* St Peter's feast day is 29 June

2 *Trier* Treves, in West Germany
9 *Campania* Naples lies within the region of Campania
13 *learned Maro* The poet Virgil (Publius Virgilius Maro) was buried in Naples in 19 B.C., and posthumously acquired some reputation as a magician. His tomb stands at the end of the promontory of Posilippo between Naples and Pozzuoli; legend ascribes the tunnel running through this promontory to his magic art

From thence to Venice, Padua, and the rest,
In midst of which a sumptuous temple stands,
That threats the stars with her aspiring top.
Thus hitherto hath Faustus spent his time.
But tell me now, what resting place is this?   20
Hast thou, as erst I did command,
Conducted me within the walls of Rome?

MEPHASTOPHILIS

Faustus, I have; and because we will not be unprovided, I
have taken up his holiness' privy chamber for our use.

FAUSTUS

I hope his holiness will bid us welcome.   25

MEPHASTOPHILIS

Tut, 'tis no matter man, we'll be bold with his good cheer.
And now, my Faustus, that thou may'st perceive
What Rome containeth to delight thee with,
Know that this city stands upon seven hills
That underprop the groundwork of the same;   30
Just through the midst runs flowing Tiber's stream,
With winding banks, that cut it in two parts;
Over the which four stately bridges lean,
That makes safe passage to each part of Rome.
Upon the bridge called Ponte Angelo   35
Erected is a castle passing strong,
Within whose walls such store of ordinance are,
And double cannons, framed of carved brass,
As match the days within one complete year;

---

16   *and the rest* B tries to be more precise with 'to the east', but there is no clear sense of
    direction

17–18   *a sumptuous temple* St Mark's in Venice; details of the mosaics and the gilded roof are
    supplied by *EFB*, and have been incorporated into the B text:
      whose frame is paved with sundry coloured stones,
      And roofed aloft with curious work in gold.
    But St Mark's has no *aspiring top*, unless the nearby campanile is intended

21   *erst* earlier

23   *Faustus, I have* From this point the A and B Texts are only occasionally similar; B's version
    of the remainder of the scene is printed in the Appendix

31–2   The lines are supplied in the B Text to supply an obvious deficiency in A (the 'stately
    bridges' must have something to lean over)

35–6   *Upon . . . strong* The Ponte Angelo was built in A.D 135 by Hadrian, whose mausoleum
    (directly facing the bridge but never standing on it) became the Castello di S. Angelo

38   *double cannons* cannons of very high calibre

Besides the gates, and high pyramides   40
Which Julius Caesar brought from Africa.

FAUSTUS

Now by the kingdoms of infernal rule,
Of Styx, Acheron, and the fiery lake
Of ever-burning Phlegethon, I swear
That I do long to see the monuments   45
And situation of bright-splendent Rome.
Come therefore, let's away.

MEPHASTOPHILIS

Nay Faustus stay, I know you'd fain see the pope,
And take some part of holy Peter's feast,
Where thou shalt see a troup of bald-pate friars,   50
Whose *summum bonum* is in belly-cheer.

FAUSTUS

Well, I am content to compass then some sport,
And by their folly make us merriment.
Then charm me that I may be invisible, to do what I please
unseen of any whilst I stay in Rome.   55

MEPHASTOPHILIS [*casts a spell on him*]

So Faustus, now do what thou wilt, thou shall not be
discerned.

Sound a sennet; enter the POPE *and the* CARDINAL OF LORRAINE
to the banquet, with FRIARS *attending*

POPE

My lord of Lorraine, will't please you draw near.

FAUSTUS

Fall to; and the devil choke you and you spare.

40–1 *pyramides . . . Africa* the obelisk that stands in front of St Peter's; it was in fact brought
from Egypt by the emperor Caligula. The plural form *pyramides* is often used for the
singular: here the extra syllable is needed for the regular pentameter
43–4 *Styx . . . Phlegethon* the rivers in Hades, the Greek underworld
46 *situation* lay-out
bright-splendent resplendent
51 *summum bonum* greatest good; in scholastic theology this is a term used to describe the
Almighty
52 *compass* take part in
59 *Fall to* get on with it
and if

POPE

How now, who's that which spake? Friars, look about.   60

1 FRIAR

Here's nobody, if it like your holiness.

POPE

My lord, here is a dainty dish was sent to me from the bishop of
Milan.

FAUSTUS

I thank you, sir.   *Snatch it*

POPE

How now, who's that which snatched the meat from me?   65
Will no man look? My lord, this dish was sent me from the
cardinal of Florence.

FAUSTUS

You say true? I'll have't.   [*Snatch it*]

POPE

What, again! My lord, I'll drink to your grace.

FAUSTUS

I'll pledge your grace.   [*Snatch the cup*]   70

LORRAINE

My lord, it may be some ghost newly crept out of purgatory
come to beg a pardon of your holiness.

POPE

It may be so; friars, prepare a dirge to lay the fury of this
ghost. Once again my lord, fall to.

The POPE *crosseth himself*

FAUSTUS

What, are you crossing of your self? Well, use that trick no   75
more, I would advise you.   *Cross again*

FAUSTUS

Well, there's the second time; aware the third! I give you fair
warning.

70   *pledge* toast
72   *pardon* papal indulgence
73   *dirge* a corruption of *dirige*, which starts the antiphon at Matins in the Office for the
      Dead; hence any requiem mass. The word is used correctly here by the pope, but the
      ritual performed is not in fact a mass but a formal cursing
74   s.d. *crosseth himself EFB* describes how the pope 'would ever be blessing and crossing
      over his mouth'

Cross again, and FAUSTUS *hits him a box of the ear,*
and they all run away

FAUSTUS

Come on Mephastophilis, what shall we do?

MEPHASTOPHILIS

Nay, I know not; we shall be cursed with bell, book, and   80
candle.

FAUSTUS

How! Bell, book, and candle; candle, book, and bell,
Forward and backward, to curse Faustus to hell.
Anon you shall hear a hog grunt, a calf bleat, and an ass
                                                        bray,
Because it is St Peter's holy day.   85

Enter all the FRIARS *to sing the Dirge*

1 FRIAR

Come brethren, let's about our business with good
devotion.

Sing this

Cursed be he that stole away his holiness' meat from the table.
          Maledicat Dominus.
Cursed be he that struck his holiness a blow on the face.   90
          Maledicat Dominus.
Cursed be he that took Friar Sandelo a blow on the pate.
          Maledicat Dominus.
Cursed be he that disturbeth our holy dirge.
          Maledicat Dominus.   95
Cursed be he that took away his holiness' wine.
          Maledicat dominus.
                    Et omnes sancti. Amen.
                    Beat the Friars, and fling fireworks among
                    them, and so Exeunt

80–1 *bell, book, and candle* At the close of the Office of Excommunication the bell is tolled,
         the bible closed, and the candle extinguished
  89 *Maledicat Dominus* May the Lord curse him
  92 *Sandelo* the name probably suggested by the friar's sandals
  98 *et omnes sancti* and all the saints

Scene 8

Enter ROBIN *and* RAFE *with a silver goblet*

ROBIN

Come Rafe, did not I tell thee we were for ever made by
this Doctor Faustus' book? *Ecce signum*! Here's a simple
purchase for horse-keepers: our horses shall eat no hay as
long as this lasts.

Enter the VINTNER

RAFE

But Robin, here comes the vintner.   5

ROBIN

Hush, I'll gull him supernaturally! Drawer, I hope all is
paid; God be with you. Come, Rafe.

VINTNER

Soft sir, a word with you. I must yet have a goblet paid
from you ere you go.

ROBIN

I a goblet, Rafe! I a goblet? I scorn you: and you are but a   10
&c . . . I a goblet? Search me.

VINTNER

I mean so, sir, with your favour.   [*Searches* ROBIN]

ROBIN

How say you now?

VINTNER

I must say somewhat to your fellow; you sir!

RAFE

Me sir! Me sir? Search your fill. Now sir, you may be   15
ashamed to burden honest men with a matter of truth.

                             [*Searches* RAFE]

VINTNER

Well, t'one of you hath this goblet about you.

Scene 8   The B Text version of this scene is printed in the Appendix

     2   *Ecce signum* behold the proof – a fairly common catchword amongst Elizabethan comic
         actors: cf. *1 Henry IV*, where Falstaff shows his 'sword hack'd like a handsaw – *ecce signum*'
         (II, iv, 168)
   2–3   *simple purchase* clear profit
     6   *gull* trick
  10–11   *but a &c* this gives the actor permission for ad-lib terms of abuse

ROBIN

You lie, drawer, 'tis afore me. Sirra you, I'll teach ye to
impeach honest men: [*to* RAFE] stand by. [*to the* VINTNER]
I'll scour you for a goblet – stand aside, you were best – I   20
charge you in the name of Belzebub – look to the goblet,
Rafe!

VINTNER

What mean you, sirra?

ROBIN

I'll tell you what I mean: [*He reads*] *Sanctobulorum
Periphrasticon* – nay, I'll tickle you, vintner – look to the   25
goblet, Rafe – *Polypragmos Belseborams framanto pacostiphos
tostis Mephastophilis, &c* . . .

> *Enter* MEPHASTOPHILIS: *sets squibs at their backs:
> they run about*

VINTNER

O nomine Domine! What mean'st thou Robin? Thou hast
no goblet.

RAFE

Peccatum peccatorum! Here's thy goblet, good Vintner.   30

ROBIN

Misericordia pro nobis! What shall I do? Good devil, forgive
me now, and I'll never rob thy library more.

> *Enter to them (again)* MEPHASTOPHILIS

MEPHASTOPHILIS

Vanish villains, th'one like an ape, an other like a bear, the
third an ass, for doing this enterprise.

> *Exit* VINTNER

Monarch of hell, under whose black survey   35
Great potentates do kneel with awful fear;
Upon whose altars thousand souls do lie;
How am I vexed with these villains' charms!

24–7 The dog-Latin marks the clowns' attempts to protect themselves from the devil
   32 s.d. *Enter to them* Boas suggests that the script must allow for alternative endings to the
       scene – but this seems unnecessary. It would be in proper medieval tradition for the devil
       to carry off the Vintner; he could then return to deal with Robin and Rafe (who, after
       all, are the real offenders)

From Constantinople am I hither come,
Only for pleasure of these damned slaves.   40

ROBIN

How, from Constantinople? You have had a great journey!
Will you take sixpence in your purse to pay for your
supper, and be gone?

MEPHASTOPHILIS

Well villains, for your presumption, I transform thee into an ape,
and thee into a dog; and so be gone!   *Exit*   45

ROBIN

How, into an ape? That's brave: I'll have fine sport with the
boys; I'll get nuts and apples enow.

RAFE

And I must be a dog.

ROBIN

I'faith, thy head will never be out of the potage pot.   *Exeunt*

Chorus 3

Enter CHORUS [WAGNER]

CHORUS

When Faustus had with pleasure ta'en the view
Of rarest things, and royal courts of kings,
He stayed his course, and so returned home;
Where such as bare his absence but with grief –
I mean his friends and nearest companions –   5
Did gratulate his safety with kind words.
And in their conference of what befell,
Touching his journey through the world and air,
They put forth questions of astrology,
Which Faustus answered with such learned skill,   10

49   *potage* porridge

Chorus 3 The B Text has no trace of this Chorus, which is obviously intended to move the play's
main action from the papal to the imperial court

As they admired and wondered at his wit.
Now is his fame spread forth in every land:
Amongst the rest the emperor is one,
Carolus the fifth, at whose palace now
Faustus is feasted 'mongst his noblemen.   15
What there he did in trial of his art
I leave untold: your eyes shall see performed.   *Exit*

Scene 9

Enter EMPEROR, FAUSTUS, *and a* KNIGHT,
with Attendants

EMPEROR

Master Doctor Faustus, I have heard strange report of thy
knowledge in the black art, how that none in my empire,
nor in the whole world, can compare with thee for the rare
effects of magic. They say thou hast a familiar spirit, by
whom thou canst accomplish what thou list! This therefore   5
is my request: that thou let me see some proof of thy skill,
that mine eyes may be witnesses to confirm what mine ears
have heard reported. And here I swear to thee, by the
honour of mine imperial crown, that whatever thou dost,
thou shalt be in no ways prejudiced or endamaged.   10

KNIGHT (*aside*)

I'faith, he looks much like a conjuror.

FAUSTUS

My gracious sovereign, though I must confess myself far
inferior to the report men have published, and nothing
answerable to the honour of your imperial majesty, yet for
that love and duty binds me thereunto, I am content to do   15
whatsoever your majesty shall command me.

EMPEROR

Then Doctor Faustus, mark what I shall say. As I was
sometime solitary set within my closet, sundry thoughts

14   *Carolus* Charles V (1519–56), whose court was at Innsbruck

Scene 9   B's much-expanded version of this scene is printed in the Appendix
18   *set* sitting

arose about the honour of mine ancestors – how they had
won by prowess such exploits, got such riches, subdued so   20
many kingdoms, as we that do succeed, or they that shall
hereafter possess our throne, shall (I fear me) never attain
to that degree of high renown and great authority. Amongst
which kings is Alexander the Great, chief spectacle of the
world's pre-eminence: 25
The bright shining of whose glorious acts
Lightens the world with his reflecting beams;
As when I hear but motion made of him,
It grieves my soul I never saw the man.
If therefore thou, by cunning of thine art,   30
Canst raise this man from hollow vaults below,
Where lies entombed this famous conqueror,
And bring with him his beauteous paramour,
Both in their right shapes, gesture, and attire
They used to wear during their time of life,   35
Thou shalt both satisfy my just desire,
And give me cause to praise thee whilst I live.

FAUSTUS
My gracious lord, I am ready to accomplish your request,
so far forth as by art and power of my spirit I am able to
perform   40

KNIGHT (*aside*)
I'faith, that's just nothing at all.

FAUSTUS
But, if it like your grace, it is not in my ability to present
before your eyes the true substantial bodies of those two
deceased princes which long since are consumed to dust.

KNIGHT (*aside*)
Ay, marry, master doctor, now there's a sign of grace in   45
you, when you will confess the truth.

FAUSTUS
But such spirits as can lively resemble Alexander and his
paramour shall appear before your grace, in that manner
that they best lived in, in their most flourishing estate:
which I doubt not shall sufficiently content your imperial   50
majesty.

24   *Alexander the Great* Alexander III of Macedon (356–323 B.C.)
28   *motion* mention
33   *paramour* probably Roxana, Alexander's wife

EMPEROR

Go to, master doctor, let me see them presently.

KNIGHT

Do you hear, master doctor? You bring Alexander and his paramour
before the emperor!

FAUSTUS

How then, sir?   55

KNIGHT

I'faith, that's as true as Diana turned me to a stag.

FAUSTUS

No sir; but when Actaeon died, he left the horns for you!
Mephastophilis, begone!

Exit MEPHASTOPHILIS

KNIGHT

Nay, and you go to conjuring I'll be gone.

Exit KNIGHT

FAUSTUS

I'll meet with you anon for interrupting me so. Here they   60
are, my gracious lord.

Enter MEPHASTOPHILIS
with ALEXANDER *and his* PARAMOUR

EMPEROR

Master doctor, I heard this lady, while she lived, had a wart
or mole in her neck; how shall I know whether it be so or
no?

FAUSTUS

Your highness may boldly go and see.   65

[*The* EMPEROR *examines the lady's neck*]

EMPEROR

Sure, these are no spirits, but the true substantial bodies of those
two deceased princes.

Exit ALEXANDER [*and his* PARAMOUR]

57 *Actaeon* As a punishment for coming upon the goddess Diana and her nymphs
   when they were bathing, Actaeon was turned into a stag, and his own hounds
   tore him to pieces

FAUSTUS

Will't please your highness now to send for the knight that
was so pleasant with me here of late?

EMPEROR

One of you call him forth.   70

Enter the KNIGHT *with a pair of horns on his head*

EMPEROR

How now sir knight? Why, I had thought thou hadst been a
bachelor, but now I see thou hast a wife that not only gives thee
horns but makes thee wear them! Feel on thy head.

KNIGHT

Thou damned wretch and execrable dog,
Bred in the concave of some monstrous rock,   75
How dar'st thou thus abuse a gentleman?
Villain I say, undo what thou hast done.

FAUSTUS

O not so fast sir, there's no haste but good. Are you
remembered how you crossed me in my conference with
the emperor? I think I have met with you for it.   80

EMPEROR

Good master doctor, at my entreaty release him; he hath
done penance sufficient.

FAUSTUS

My gracious lord, not so much for the injury he offered me
here in your presence, as to delight you with some mirth,
hath Faustus worthily requited this injurious knight; which   85
being all I desire, I am content to release him of his horns.
And, sir knight, hereafter speak well of scholars: Mephastophilis, transform him straight. Now my good lord, having
done my duty, I humbly take my leave.

72–3   *wife . . . wear them* It was an old joke that the cuckolded husband would grow horns to
       publish his shame
  75   *Bred . . . rock* cf. 2 *Tamburlaine,* III,ii, 89: 'Fenc'd with the concave of some monstrous
       rock'
78–9   *Are you remembered* Have you forgotten

EMPEROR

Farewell master doctor; yet ere you go, expect from me a   90
bounteous reward.

Exit EMPEROR [*and his Attendants*]

FAUSTUS

Now Mephastophilis, the restless course
That time doth run with calm and silent foot,
Shortening my days and thread of vital life,
Calls for the payment of my latest years;   95
Therefore, sweet Mephastophilis, let us make haste to
                                                 Wittenberg.

MEPHASTOPHILIS

What, will you go on horseback, or on foot?

FAUSTUS

Nay, till I am past this fair and pleasant green, I'll walk on
foot.

Scene 10

Enter [*to them*] *a* HORSE-COURSER

HORSE-COURSER

I have been all this day seeking one Master Fustian: 'mass,
see where he is! God save you, master doctor.

FAUSTUS

What, horse-courser: you are well met.

HORSE-COURSER

Do you hear, sir; I have brought you forty dollars for your
horse.   5

---

94 *thread of vital life* The image of life as a single thread comes from Greek mythology
95 *payment* The idea of death as a debt owed to nature is a commonplace (cf. *Macbeth*,
    V,ix, 5: 'Your son, my lord, has paid a soldier's debt'); but it is revitalized here by Faustus'
    predicament
    latest last

Scene 10 The B Text version of this scene is printed in the Appendix
  s.d *Horse-courser* Horse-dealer; a reputation for dishonesty has always attached to such
       traders
    1 *Fustian* the Horse-courser's mispronunciation of 'Faustus'– and perhaps a suggestion
       that the role was once doubled with that of the Clown who in Scene 4 commented that
       Wagner spoke 'Dutch fustian'

FAUSTUS

I cannot sell him so: if thou lik'st him for fifty, take him.

HOURSE-COURSER

Alas sir, I have no more. I pray you speak for me.

MEPHASTOPHILIS

I pray you let him have him; he is an honest fellow, and he
has a great charge – neither wife nor child.

FAUSTUS

Well; come, give me your money; my boy will deliver him   10
to you. But I must tell you one thing before you have him:
ride him not into the water at any hand.

HORSE-COURSER

Why sir, will he not drink of all waters?

FAUSTUS

O yes, he will drink of all waters, but ride him not into the
water. Ride him over hedge or ditch, or where thou wilt,   15
but not into the water.

HORSE-COURSER

Well sir. Now am I made man for ever: I'll not leave my
horse for forty! If he had but the quality of hey ding ding,
hey ding ding, I'd make a brave living on him! He has a
buttock as slick as an eel. Well, God b'y sir; your boy will   20
deliver him me. But hark ye sir, if my horse be sick, or ill at
ease, if I bring his water to you, you'll tell me what it is?

Exit HORSE-COURSER

FAUSTUS

Away, you villain! What, dost think I am a horse-doctor?
What art thou, Faustus, but a man condemned to die?
Thy fatal time doth draw to final end.   25

---

12 *not into the water* Running water dissolves a witch's spell
    at any hand whatever happens
13 *drink of all waters* go anywhere
17 *leave* part with
18 *for forty* for any amount of money
    quality of hey ding ding The Horse-courser seems to be wishing that the horse were a
    stallion, not a gelding; cf. Nashe, *Have With You to Saffron Walden* (1596): 'Yea, Madam
    Gabriele, are you such an old ierker? then Hey ding a ding, vp with your perticoate, haue
    at your plum-tree' (McKerrow iii, p. 113)
22 *his water* his urine (for diagnosis)

Despair doth drive distrust unto my thoughts:
Confound these passions with a quiet sleep.
Tush, Christ did call the thief upon the cross;
Then rest thee, Faustus, quiet in conceit.

Sleep in his chair

Enter HORSE-COURSER *all wet, crying*

HORSE-COURSER

Alas, alas, Doctor Fustian, quoth 'a: 'mass, Doctor Lopus   30
was never such a doctor! H'as given me a purgation, h'as
purged me of forty dollars! I shall never see them more. But
yet, like an ass as I was, I would not be ruled by him; for he
bade me I should ride him into no water. Now I, thinking
my horse had had some rare quality that he would not have   35
had me known of, I, like a vent'rous youth, rid him into the
deep pond at the town's end. I was no sooner in the middle
of the pond, but my horse vanished away, and I sat upon a
bottle of hay, never so near drowning in my life! But I'll
seek out my doctor, and have my forty dollars again, or I'll   40
make it the dearest horse. O, yonder is his snipper-snapper!
Do you hear, you hey-pass, where's your master?

MEPHASTOPHILIS

Why sir, what would you? You cannot speak with him.

HORSE-COURSER

But I will speak with him.

MEPHASTOPHILIS

Why, he's fast asleep; come some other time.   45

HORSE-COURSER

I'll speak with him now, or I'll break his glass-windows
about his ears.

MEPHASTOPHILIS

I tell thee, he has not slept this eight nights.

---

28 *Christ . . . cross* St Luke's Gospel tells of Christ's words of comfort to the crucified thief:
'This day shall thou be with me in paradise' (xxiii, 43)

29 *in conceit* in this thought

30 *Doctor Lopus* This joke must have found its way into the text after the execution, in
February 1594, of Roderigo Lopez, Queen Elizabeth's personal physician, who was accused
of plotting to poison Her Majesty

39 *bottle* truss

42 *hey-pass* a conjuror's 'magic' catchphrase

46 *glass-windows* spectacles

HORSE-COURSER

And he has not slept this eight weeks I'll speak with him.   50

MEPHASTOPHILIS

See where he is, fast asleep.

HORSE-COURSER

Ay, this is he; God save ye master doctor, master doctor, master Doctor Fustian, forty dollars, forty dollars for a bottle of hay.

MEPHASTOPHILIS

Why, thou seest he hears thee not.   55

HORSE-COURSER

So ho ho; so ho ho.   *Halloo in his ear*

No, will you not wake? I'll make you wake ere I go.

Pull him by the leg, and pull it away

Alas, I am undone! What shall I do?

FAUSTUS

O my leg, my leg! Help, Mephastophilis! Call the officers! My leg, my leg!   60

MEPHASTOPHILIS

Come villain, to the constable.

HORSE-COURSER

O Lord, sir! Let me go, and I'll give you forty dollars more.

MEPHASTOPHILIS

Where be they?

HORSE-COURSER

I have none about me: come to my ostry and I'll give them you.   65

MEPHASTOPHILIS

Begone quickly!   HORSE-COURSER *runs away*

FAUSTUS

What, is he gone? Farewell he: Faustus has his leg again, and the horse-courser – I take it – a bottle of hay for his labour! Well, this trick shall cost him forty dollars more.

56 *So ho ho* the huntsman's cry when he catches sight of the quarry
64 *ostry* hostelry, inn

Enter WAGNER

How now Wagner, what's the news with thee?   70

WAGNER

Sir, the Duke of Vanholt doth earnestly entreat your
company.

FAUSTUS

The Duke of Vanholt! An honourable gentleman, to whom
I must be no niggard of my cunning. Come Mephastophilis,
let's away to him.   *Exeunt*   75

Scene 11

[FAUSTUS *and* MEPHASTOPHILIS *return to the stage.*]
Enter to them the DUKE *and the* DUCHESS;
the DUKE *speaks*

DUKE

Believe me, master doctor, this merriment hath much
pleased me.

FAUSTUS

My gracious Lord, I am glad it contents you so well: but it
may be, madam, you take no delight in this; I have heard
that great-bellied women do long for some dainties or   5
other – what is it, madam? Tell me, and you shall have it.

DUCHESS

Thanks, good master doctor; and for I see your courteous
intent to pleasure me, I will not hide from you the thing my
heart desires. And were it now summer, as it is January and
the dead of winter, I would desire no better meat than a   10
dish of ripe grapes.

FAUSTUS

Alas madam, that's nothing! Mephastophilis, begone!

Exit MEPHASTOPHILIS

Scene 11 In the B Text this scene is expanded, but not substantially altered. It is preceded by a
tavern scene, where the clowns narrate some of the Doctor's trickeries, and followed by
an episode which merges the court and the tavern so that Faustus can play another trick
on the clowns

s.d. *Enter to them* On the printed page this seems to be a clumsy way of linking two episodes,
but on the stage there is no problem

Were it a greater thing than this, so it would content you, you should have it.

Enter MEPHASTOPHILIS *with the grapes*

Here they be, madam; will't please you taste on them?   15

DUKE

Believe me, master doctor, this makes me wonder above the rest: that being in the dead time of winter, and in the month of January, how you should come by these grapes?

FAUSTUS

If it like your grace, the year is divided into two circles over the whole world, that when it is here winter with us, in the   20 contrary circle it is summer with them, as in India, Saba, and farther countries in the east; and by means of a swift spirit that I have, I had them brought hither, as ye see. How do you like them, madam; be they good?

DUCHESS

Believe me, master doctor, they be the best grapes that ere I   25 tasted in my life before.

FAUSTUS

I am glad they content you so, madam.

DUKE

Come madam, let us in, where you must well reward this learned man for the great kindness he hath showed to you.

DUCHESS

And so I will my lord; and whilst I live, rest beholding for   30 this courtesy.

FAUSTUS

I humbly thank your grace.

DUKE

Come, master doctor, follow us, and receive your reward.

Exeunt

19   *two circles* The explanation is confusing. The relevant circles would be the northern and
      southern hemispheres, but the author appears to be thinking in terms of east and west;
      EFB evades the matter while providing the detail of the twice-yearly fruit
21   *Saba* Sheba; in modern times, this is the Yemen

[Chorus 4]

Enter WAGNER *solus*

WAGNER
I think my master means to die shortly,
For he hath given to me all his goods!
And yet methinks, if that death were near,
He would not banquet, and carouse, and swill,
Amongst the students, as even now he doth,   5
Who are at supper with such belly-cheer,
As Wagner ne'er beheld in all his life.
See where they come: belike the feast is ended.   [*Exit*]

Scene 12

Enter FAUSTUS [*and* MEPHASTOPHILIS],
with two or three SCHOLARS

1 SCHOLAR
Master Doctor Faustus, since our conference about fair
ladies, which was the beautifullest in all the world, we have
determined with ourselves that Helen of Greece was the
admirablest lady that ever lived. Therefore, master doctor,
if you will do us that favour as to let us see that peerless   5
dame of Greece, whom all the world admires for majesty,
we should think ourselves much beholding unto you.

FAUSTUS
Gentlemen for that I know your friendship is unfeigned,
And Faustus' custom is not to deny
The just requests of those that wish him well,   10
You shall behold that peerless dame of Greece,

Chorus   Again, the direction for Wagner's entrance suggests that the choric figure doubled
with the role of Faustus' servant
1–8   In place of these lines, B gives Wagner a prose speech containing the gist of A's verse

Scene 12   The A and B versions of this scene are closely related; but B is markedly inferior to
A, reading like a poor memorial reconstruction of the Scholars' lines, but having a re-
written speech for the Old Man
3   *Helen of Greece* Helen (who was married to Menelaus, king of Sparta) was given to Paris
as a reward for judging the contest of three goddesses
8–15   as prose in A

No otherways for pomp and majesty
Than when Sir Paris crossed the seas with her,
And brought the spoils to rich Dardania.
Be silent then, for danger is in words.   15

Music sounds, and HELEN *passeth over the stage*

2 SCHOLAR
Too simple is my wit to tell her praise,
Whom all the world admires for majesty.
3 SCHOLAR
No marvel though the angry Greeks pursued
With ten years' war the rape of such a queen,
Whose heavenly beauty passeth all compare.   20
1 SCHOLAR
Since we have seen the pride of Nature's works,
And only paragon of excellence,
Let us depart; and for this glorious deed
Happy and blest be Faustus evermore.
FAUSTUS
Gentlemen farewell; the same I wish to you.   25

Exeunt SCHOLARS

Enter an OLD MAN

OLD MAN
Ah Doctor Faustus, that I might prevail

---

14 *Dardania* Troy; in fact the city built by Dardanus on the Hellespont, but the name is
    often transferred to Troy
15 s.d. *passeth over* It would appear that the character was instructed to move from one side of
    the yard, across the stage, and out at the other side of the yard, instead of entering by the stage
    doors (cf. Allardyce Nicoll, 'Passing Over the Stage', *Shakespeare Survey*, XII [1959], pp. 47–55)
16–24 In the B Text the Scholars' comments are as follows:
       2 SCHOLAR
       Was this fair Helen, whose admired worth
       Made Greece with ten years' war afflict poor Troy?
       3 SCHOLAR
       Too simple is my wit to tell her worth,
       Whom all the world admires for majesty.
       1 SCHOLAR
       Now we have seen the pride of Nature's work,
       We'll take our leaves, and for this blessed sight
       Happy and blest be Faustus evermore.
26–37 The Old Man's speech is oddly strained: a 'goal' cannot 'conduct', and 'commiseration'
    does not 'expel'; the speech seems to have been re-written for the B Text – see the Appendix

[84]

To guide thy steps unto the way of life,
By which sweet path thou may'st attain the goal
That shall conduct thee to celestial rest.
Break heart, drop blood, and mingle it with tears,　　　　30
Tears falling from repentant heaviness
Of thy most vile and loathsome filthiness,
The stench whereof corrupts the inward soul
With such flagitious crimes of heinous sins,
As no commiseration may expel;　　　　35
But mercy, Faustus, of thy saviour sweet,
Whose blood alone must wash away thy guilt.

FAUSTUS

Where art thou Faustus? Wretch, what hast thou done!
Damned art thou Faustus, damned; despair and die!

MEPHASTOPHILIS *gives him a dagger*

Hell calls for right, and with a roaring voice　　　　40
Says, 'Faustus, come: thine hour is come'!
And Faustus will come to do thee right.

OLD MAN

Ah stay, good Faustus, stay thy desperate steps!
I see an angel hovers o'er thy head,
And with a vial full of precious grace　　　　45
Offers to pour the same into thy soul!
Then call for mercy, and avoid despair.

FAUSTUS

Ah my sweet friend, I feel thy words
To comfort my distressed soul;
Leave me awhile to ponder on my sins.　　　　50

OLD MAN

I go, sweet Faustus; but with heavy cheer,
Fearing the ruin of thy hopeless soul.　　　　[*Exit*]

FAUSTUS

Accursed Faustus, where is mercy now?
I do repent, and yet I do despair:
Hell strives with grace for conquest in my breast!　　　　55
What shall I do to shun the snares of death?

MEPHASTOPHILIS

Thou traitor, Faustus: I arrest thy soul
For disobedience to my sovereign lord.

[85]

Revolt, or I'll in piecemeal tear thy flesh.

FAUSTUS

Sweet Mephastophilis, entreat thy lord   60
To pardon my unjust presumption;
And with my blood again I will confirm
My former vow I made to Lucifer.

MEPHASTOPHILIS

Do it then quickly, with unfeigned heart,
Lest greater danger do attend thy drift.   65

FAUSTUS

Torment, sweet friend, that base and crooked age
That durst dissuade me from thy Lucifer,
With greatest torments that our hell affords.

MEPHASTOPHILIS

His faith is great, I cannot touch his soul,
But what I may afflict his body with,   70
I will attempt – which is but little worth.

FAUSTUS

One thing, good servant, let me crave of thee,
To glut the longing of my heart's desire:
That I might have unto my paramour
That heavenly Helen which I saw of late,   75
Whose sweet embracings may extinguish clean
These thoughts that do dissuade me from my vow:
And keep mine oath I made to Lucifer.

MEPHASTOPHILIS

Faustus, this, or what else thou shalt desire,
Shall be performed in twinkling of an eye.   80

Enter HELEN

FAUSTUS

Was this the face that launched a thousand ships,
And burnt the topless towers of Ilium?

---

59 *Revolt* Turn again to your allegiance
65 *drift* drifting; also purpose
81–100 In these lines Marlowe is repeating his own memorable phrases:
       Helen, whose beauty summoned Greece to arms,
       And drew a thousand ships to Tenedos.
                         2 Tamburlaine, II, iv, 87–8

Sweet Helen, make me immortal with a kiss:
Her lips sucks forth my soul, see where it flies!
Come Helen, come, give me my soul again.   85
Here will I dwell, for heaven be in these lips,
And all is dross that is not Helena!

Enter OLD MAN

I will be Paris, and for love of thee,
Instead of Troy shall Wittenberg be sacked;
And I will combat with weak Menelaus,   90
And wear thy colours on my plumed crest:
Yea, I will wound Achilles in the heel,
And then return to Helen for a kiss.
O thou art fairer than the evening air,
Clad in the beauty of a thousand stars,   95
Brighter art thou than flaming Jupiter
When he appeared to hapless Semele;
More lovely than the monarch of the sky
In wanton Arethusa's azured arms;
And none but thou shalt be my paramour.   100

Exeunt [FAUSTUS *and* HELEN]

OLD MAN
Accursed Faustus, miserable man,
That from thy soul exclud'st the grace of heaven,
And fliest the throne of His tribunal seat!

And he'll make me immortal with a kiss.

Dido, IV, iv, 123

So thou wouldst prove as true as Paris did,
Would, as fair Troy was, Carthage might be sacked,
And I be called a second Helena.

Dido, V,1, 146–8 82

82 *Ilium* Troy

88 s.d. This direction and the Old Man's final speech (101–9) are omitted in the B Text

92 *wound . . . heel* Achilles was invulnerable apart from one of his heels – where he was shot by Paris

96–7 *flaming . . . Semele* The sight of Jupiter in all his divine splendour was too much for mortal eyes, and Semele was consumed by the fire of his brightness

98–9 *monarch . . . arms* Arethusa was a nymph who was changed into a fountain after bathing in the river Alpheus and exciting the river-god's passion; Alpheus is said to have been related to the sun

Enter the DEVILS

Satan begins to sift me with his pride,
As in this furnace God shall try my faith.   105
My faith, vile hell, shall triumph over thee!
Ambitious fiends, see how the heavens smiles
At your repulse, and laughs your state to scorn.
Hence hell, for hence I fly unto my God.   *Exeunt*

Scene 13

Enter FAUSTUS *with the* SCHOLARS

FAUSTUS

Ah gentlemen!

1 SCHOLAR

What ails Faustus?

FAUSTUS

Ah my sweet chamber-fellow, had I lived with thee, then
had I lived still; but now I die eternally. Look, comes he
not, comes he not?   5

2 SCHOLAR

What means Faustus?

3 SCHOLAR

Belike he is grown into some sickness, by being over-
solitary.

1 SCHOLAR

If it be so, we'll have physicians to cure him; 'tis but a
surfeit: never fear, man.   10

FAUSTUS

A surfeit of deadly sin, that hath damned both body and
soul.

---

104   *sift* Cf. St Luke's Gospel xxii, 3: 'Satan hath desired to have you, that he may sift you as
      wheat'

107   *the heavens* the celestial beings who inhabit the extra-terrestial spheres of the geocentric
      universe.
      smiles A singular verb following a plural subject is not uncommon in sixteenth-century
      literature

scene 13   B opens this scene with the arrival of the devils – Lucifer, Belzebub, and Mephasto-
      philis – who have come to witness Faustus' end; see the Appendix

2 SCHOLAR

Yet Faustus, look up to heaven; remember God's mercies are infinite.

FAUSTUS

But Faustus' offence can ne'er be pardoned! The serpent 15
that tempted Eve may be saved, but not Faustus. Ah
gentlemen, hear me with patience, and tremble not at my
speeches, though my heart pants and quivers to remember
that I have been a student here these thirty years – O would
I had never seen Wittenberg, never read book – and what 20
wonders I have done, all Wittenberg can witness – yea, all
the world; for which Faustus hath lost both Germany and
the world – yea, heaven itself – heaven, the seat of God, the
throne of the blessed, the kingdom of joy; and must remain
in hell for ever – hell, ah, hell for ever! Sweet friends, what 25
shall become of Faustus, being in hell for ever?

3 SCHOLAR

Yet Faustus, call on God.

FAUSTUS

On God, whom Faustus hath abjured? On God, whom
Faustus hath blasphemed? Ah my God – I would weep, but
the devil draws in my tears! gush forth blood instead of 30
tears – yea, life and soul! O, he stays my tongue! I would lift
up my hands, but see, they hold them, they hold them!

ALL

Who, Faustus?

FAUSTUS

Lucifer and Mephastophilis! Ah gentlemen, I gave them my soul
for my cunning. 35

ALL

God forbid!

FAUSTUS

God forbade it indeed, but Faustus hath done it: for the
vain pleasure of four-and-twenty years hath Faustus lost

---

30 *draws in my tears* 'No not so much as their eyes are able to shed tears (thretten and torture
them as ye please) while first they repent (God not permitting them to dissemble their
obstinacie in so horrible a crime)', *Daemonologie*, by James VI and I (Edinburgh, 1597),
p. 81

31 *stays* holds back

37–8 *for the vain* B (for vain A)

eternal joy and felicity! I writ them a bill with mine own blood, the date is expired, the time will come, and he will fetch me. 40

1 SCHOLAR

Why did not Faustus tell us of this before, that divines might have prayed for thee?

FAUSTUS

Oft have I thought to have done so, but the devil threatened to tear me in pieces if I named God, to fetch both body and 45 soul, if I once gave ear to divinity; and now 'tis too late! Gentlemen away, lest you perish with me.

2 SCHOLAR

O what shall we do to save Faustus?

3 SCHOLAR

God will strengthen me. I will stay with Faustus.

1 SCHOLAR

Tempt not God, sweet friend, but let us into the next room, 50 and there pray for him.

FAUSTUS

Ay, pray for me, pray for me; and what noise soever ye hear, come not unto me, for nothing can rescue me.

2 SCHOLAR

Pray thou, and we will pray, that God may have mercy upon thee. 55

FAUSTUS

Gentlemen, farewell. If I live till morning, I'll visit you; if not, Faustus is gone to hell.

ALL

Faustus, farewell.   *Exeunt* SCHOLARS
                    The clock strikes eleven

FAUSTUS

Ah Faustus,
Now hast thou but one bare hour to live, 60
And then thou must be damned perpetually.

48   *to save Faustus* B (to Faustus A)
58   *Farewell* See the Appendix for the B Text's insertion at this point

Stand still, you ever-moving spheres of heaven,
That time may cease, and midnight never come.
Fair Nature's eye, rise, rise again, and make
Perpetual day, or let this hour be but   65
A year, a month, a week, a natural day,
That Faustus may repent and save his soul.
O lente, lente currite noctis equi!
The stars move still, time runs, the clock will strike,
The devil will come, and Faustus must be damned.   70
O I'll leap up to my God! Who pulls me down?
See, see where Christ's blood streams in the firmament!
One drop would save my soul, half a drop: ah my Christ –
Ah, rend not my heart for naming of my Christ;
Yet will I call on him – O spare me, Lucifer!   75
Where is it now? 'Tis gone: and see where God
Stretcheth out his arm, and bends his ireful brows!
Mountains and hills, come, come and fall on me,
And hide me from the heavy wrath of God.
No, no?   80
Then will I headlong run into the earth:
Earth, gape! O no, it will not harbour me.
You stars that reigned at my nativity,

62–7 Cf. *Edward II*, V,i, 64–8:

> Continue ever, thou celestial sun;
> Let never silent night possess this clime:
> Stand still, you watches of the element;
> All times and seasons, rest you at a stay,
> That Edward may be still fair England's king.

68 'Go slowly, slowly, you horses of the night': the play's final irony; the line is from Ovid's *Amores*, I, xiii, 40, where the poet longs for never-ending night in his mistress' arms

71 *leap up . . . down* the titlepage of the 1604 edition depicts Faustus' position emblematically

76 *it* the vision of Christ's blood; the momentary yielding to terror and the devil banishes even this hope of salvation

78–9 'And they shall say to the mountains: Cover us; and to the hills, Fall on us', Hosea x, 8 (see also Revelations vi, 16; and St Luke xxiii, 3). The Usurer in *A Looking Glass for London* has the same idea:

> Hell gapes for me, heaven will not hold my soule,
> You mountaines shroude me from the God of truth . . .
> Cover me hills, and shroude me from the Lord.
>
> ll. 2054–5, 9

83–9 *You . . . heaven* Faustus prays the stars, whose positions at his birth ordained this fate, to suck him up into a cloud, as a fog or mist is drawn up, and then in a storm expel his

Whose influence hath allotted death and hell,
Now draw up Faustus like a foggy mist   85
Into the entrails of yon labouring cloud,
That when you vomit forth into the air
My limbs may issue from your smoky mouths,
So that my soul may but ascend to heaven.

                          The watch strikes

Ah, half the hour is past: 'twill all be past anon.   90
O God, if thou wilt not have mercy on my soul,
Yet for Christ's sake, whose blood hath ransomed me,
Impose some end to my incessant pain:
Let Faustus live in hell a thousand years,
A hundred thousand, and at last be saved.   95
O, no end is limited to damned souls!
Why wert thou not a creature wanting soul?
Or why is this immortal that thou hast?
Ah, Pythagoras' *metempsychosis* – were that true,
This soul should fly from me, and I be changed   100
Unto some brutish beast:
All beasts are happy, for when they die,
Their souls are soon dissolved in elements;
But mine must live still to be plagued in hell.
Cursed be the parents that engendered me: 105
No Faustus, curse thy self, curse Lucifer,
That hath deprived thee of the joys of heaven!

                       The clock striketh twelve

O it strikes, it strikes! Now body, turn to air,
Or Lucifer will bear thee quick to hell.

                        Thunder and lightning

O soul, be changed into little water drops,   110
And fall into the ocean, ne'er be found.
My God, my God, look not so fierce on me!

---

body in order that his soul may be saved. Cf. *1 Tamburlaine*, IV, ii, 33: 'Smile, stars that reigned at my nativity'

99   *Pythagoras metempsychosis* the theory of the transmigration of souls, attributed to Pythagoras, whereby the human soul at the death of the body took on some other form of life

109   *quick* living

Enter DEVILS

Adders and serpents, let me breathe awhile!
Ugly hell gape not! Come not, Lucifer!
I'll burn my books – ah, Mephastophilis!   115

Exeunt with him

[EPILOGUE]

Enter CHORUS

Cut is the branch that might have grown full straight,
And burned is Apollo's laurel bough,
That sometime grew within this learned man.
Faustus is gone! Regard his hellish fall,
Whose fiendful fortune may exhort the wise   5
Only to wonder at unlawful things:
Whose deepness doth entice such forward wits,
To practise more than heavenly power permits.   [*Exit*]

Terminat hora diem, terminat author opus.

---

115 *burn my books* All magicians who renounced their art made a solemn act of disposing
of their magic books; cf. *The Tempest*, V,i,56–7: 'deeper than did ever plummet sound I'll
drown my book'

115 s.d. *Exeunt with him* The B Text adds a macabre scene where the Scholars discover Faustus'
mangled body (see the Appendix). Both texts conclude with an Epilogue, in the tradition
of the Morality Plays

2 *Apollo's laurel bough* the wreath of the poet (in this case, conjuror – see scene 3, line 33) laureate
Terminat . . . opus The hour ends the day, the author ends his works. The origin is unknown,
and it seems likely that the motto, with the final emblem, was appended by the printer and
not by Marlowe
The Latin motto is followed by another printer's device – McKerrow 313: 'Framed device of
Justice striking a bushel of corn; with SUCH AS I MAKE. SUCH WILL I TAKE'

APPENDIX

Scenes from the B Text: sometimes these are straightforward additions to the play presented in the A Text; in other cases, the A scenes have been substantially re-worked. The scenes in the Appendix are identified by the numbers of the A Text scenes which they replace or augment.

Scene 4

Enter WAGNER *and the* CLOWN

WAGNER

Come hither, sirra boy.

CLOWN

Boy? O disgrace to my person: Zounds, boy in your face, you have seen many boys with beards, I am sure.

WAGNER

Sirra, hast thou no comings in?

CLOWN

Yes, and goings out too, you may see sir.

WAGNER

Alas poor slave, see how poverty jests in his nakedness. I know the villain's out of service, and so hungry, that I know he would give his soul to the devil, for a shoulder of mutton, tho' it were blood raw.

CLOWN

Not so neither! I had need to have it well roasted, and good sauce to it, if I pay so dear, I can tell you.

WAGNER

Sirra, wilt thou be my man and wait on me? And I will make thee go like *Qui mihi discipulus*.

CLOWN

What, in verse?

WAGNER

No slave, in beaten silk and stavesacre.

CLOWN

Stavesacre? That's good to kill vermin: then belike if I serve you, I shall be lousy.

WAGNER

Why, so thou shalt be, whether thou dost it or no: for sirra, if thou dost not presently bind thy self to me for seven years, I'll turn all the lice about thee into familiars, and make them tear thee in pieces.

CLOWN

Nay sir, you may save yourself a labour, for they are as familiar with me, as if they paid for their meat and drink, I can tell you.

WAGNER

Well sirra, leave your jesting, and take these guilders.

CLOWN

Yes, marry sir; and I thank you too.

WAGNER

So; now thou art to be at an hour's warning, whensoever, and wheresoever the devil shall fetch thee.

CLOWN

Here, take your guilders; I'll none of 'em.

WAGNER

Not I; thou art pressed! Prepare thyself, for I will presently raise up two devils to carry thee away: Banio, Belcher!

CLOWN

Belcher? and Belcher come here, I'll belch him: I am not afraid of a devil.

Enter TWO DEVILS

WAGNER

How now, sir; will you serve me now?

CLOWN

Ay, good Wagner; take away the devil, then.

WAGNER

Spirits, away! Now sirra, follow me.

CLOWN

I will, sir! But hark you, master – will you teach me this conjuring occupation?

WAGNER

Ay sirra, I'll teach thee to turn thyself to a dog, or a cat, or a mouse, or a rat, or anything.

CLOWN

A dog, or a cat, or a mouse, or a rat? O brave, Wagner!

WAGNER

Villain, call me Master Wagner; and see that you walk attentively, and let your right eye be always diametrally fixed upon my left heel, that thou may'st, 'Quasi vestigias nostras insistere'.

CLOWN

Well sir, I warrant you.   *Exeunt*

Scene 6

Enter the CLOWN [ROBIN]

ROBIN

What, Dick, look to the horses there till I come again. I have gotten one of Doctor Faustus' conjuring books, and now we'll have such knavery as 't passes.

Enter DICK

DICK

What, Robin, you must come away and walk the horses.

ROBIN

I walk the horses! I scorn 't, i'faith. I have other matters in hand. Let the horses walk themselves and they will. [*Reads*] 'A *per se* a, t. h. e. the; o *per se* o; deny orgon, gorgon'. Keep further from me, O thou illiterate and unlearned ostler.

DICK

'Snails, what hast thou got there? A book! Why, thou canst not tell ne'er a word on't.

ROBIN

That thou shalt see presently. Keep out of the circle, I say, lest I send you into the ostry with a vengeance.

DICK

That's like, 'faith. You had best leave your foolery, for an my master come, he'll conjure you i'faith.

ROBIN

My master conjure me? I'll tell thee what, an my master come here, I'll clap as fair a pair of horns on's head as ere thou saw'st in thy life.

DICK

Thou needst not do that, for my mistress hath done it.

ROBIN

Ay, there be of us here that have waded as deep into matters as other men, if they were disposed to talk.

DICK

> A plague take you. I thought you did not sneak up and down after her for nothing. But I prithee tell me, in good sadness Robin, is that a conjuring book?

ROBIN

> Do but speak what thou'st have me to do, and I'll do't! If thou'st dance naked, put off thy clothes and I'll conjure thee about presently. Or if thou'st go but to the tavern with me, I'll give thee white wine, red wine, claret wine, sack, muscadine, malmesy, and whippincrust – hold belly hold – and we'll not pay one penny for it.

DICK

> O brave! Prithee let's to it presently, for I am as dry as a dog.

ROBIN

> Come then, let's away.   *Exeunt*

Scene 7

MEPHOSTOPHILIS

> Nay stay my Faustus, I know you'd see the pope
> And take some part of holy Peter's feast,
> The which this day with high solemnity,
> This day is held through Rome and Italy,
> In honour of the pope's triumphant victory.

FAUSTUS

> Sweet Mephostophilis, thou pleasest me.
> Whilst I am here on earth, let me be cloyed
> With all things that delight the heart of man.
> My four and twenty years of liberty
> I'll spend in pleasure and in dalliance,
> That Faustus' name, whilst this bright frame doth stand,
> May be admired through the furthest land.

MEPHOSTOPHILIS

> 'Tis well said Faustus; come then, stand by me,
> And thou shalt see them come immediately.

FAUSTUS

> Nay, stay, my gentle Mephostophilis,
> And grant me my request, and then I go.

Thou know'st within the compass of eight days
We view'd the face of heaven, of earth and hell.
So high our dragons soar'd into the air,
That looking down the earth appeared to me,
No bigger than my hand in quantity.
There did we view the kingdoms of the world,
And what might please mine eye, I there beheld.
Then in this show let me an actor be,
That this proud pope may Faustus' coming see.

MEPHOSTOPHILIS
Let it be so, my Faustus, but first stay,
And view their triumphs, as they pass this way.
And then devise what best contents thy mind,
By cunning in thine art to cross the pope,
Or dash the pride of this solemnity;
To make his monks and abbots stand like apes,
And point like antics at his triple crown:
To beat the beads about the friars' pates,
Or clap huge horns upon the cardinals' heads:
Or any villainy thou canst devise,
And I'll perform it Faustus: hark, they come:
This day shall make thee be admired in Rome.

Enter the CARDINALS *and Bishops, some bearing croziers, some*
the pillars; monks and friars singing their procession.
Then the POPE *and* RAYMOND *King of Hungary,*
with BRUNO *led in chains*

POPE
Cast down our footstool.
RAYMOND   Saxon Bruno stoop,
Whilst on thy back his holiness ascends
Saint Peter's chair and state pontifical.

BRUNO
Proud Lucifer, that state belongs to me:
But thus I fall to Peter, not to thee.

POPE
To me and Peter, shalt thou grovelling lie,
And crouch before the papal dignity.
Sound trumpets then, for thus Saint Peter's heir,
From Bruno's back ascends Saint Peter's chair.

A flourish while he ascends

Thus, as the gods, creep on with feet of wool,
Long ere with iron hands they punish men,
So shall our sleeping vengeance now arise,
And smite with death thy hated enterprise.
Lord cardinals of France and Padua,
Go forthwith to our holy consistory,
And read amongst the statutes decretal,
What by the holy council held at Trent,
The sacred synod hath decreed for him,
That doth assume the papal government,
Without election, and a true consent:
Away and bring us word with speed.

1 CARDINAL

    We go my Lord.   *Exeunt* CARDINALS

POPE

    Lord Raymond.

FAUSTUS

    Go haste thee, gentle Mephostophilis,
    Follow the cardinals to the consistory;
    And as they turn their superstitious books,
    Strike them with sloth, and drowsy idleness;
    And make them sleep so sound, that, in their shapes,
    Thyself and I may parley with this pope,
    This proud confronter of the emperor;
    And in despite of all his holiness
    Restore this Bruno to his liberty,
    And bear him to the states of Germany.

MEPHOSTOPHILIS

    Faustus, I go.

FAUSTUS

    Dispatch it soon,
    The pope shall curse that Faustus came to Rome.
               Exeunt FAUSTUS *and* MEPHOSTOPHILIS

BRUNO

    Pope Adrian let me have some right of law,
    I was elected by the emperor.

POPE

    We will depose the emperor for that deed,
    And curse the people that submit to him;
    Both he and thou shalt stand excommunicate,

And interdict from church's privilege,
And all society of holy men:
He grows too proud in his authority,
Lifting his lofty head above the clouds,
And like a steeple overpeers the church.
But we'll pull down his haughty insolence:
And as pope Alexander our progenitor,
Trod on the neck of German Frederick,
Adding this golden sentence to our praise:
That Peter's heirs should tread on emperors,
And walk upon the dreadful adder's back,
Treading the lion and the dragon down,
And fearless spurn the killing basilisk:
So will we quell that haughty schismatic,
And by authority apostolical
Depose him from his regal government.

BRUNO

Pope Julius swore to princely Sigismond,
For him, and the succeeding popes of Rome,
To hold the emperors their lawful lords.

POPE

Pope Julius did abuse the church's rites,
And therefore none of his decrees can stand.
Is not all power on earth bestowed on us?
And therefore tho' we would we cannot err.
Behold this silver belt whereto is fixed
Seven golden seals fast sealed with seven seals,
In token of our seven-fold power from heaven,
To bind or loose, lock fast, condemn, or judge,
Resign, or seal, or what so pleaseth us.
Then he and thou, and all the world shall stoop,
Or be assured of our dreadful curse,
To light as heavy as the pains of hell.

Enter FAUSTUS *and* MEPHOSTOPHILIS *like the Cardinals*

MEPHOSTOPHILIS

Now tell me Faustus, are we not fitted well?

FAUSTUS

Yes Mephostophilis, and two such cardinals
Ne'er served a holy pope, as we shall do.
But whilst they sleep within the consistory,

Let us salute his reverend fatherhood.

RAYMOND

Behold my lord, the cardinals are returned.

POPE

Welcome grave fathers, answer presently,
What have our holy council there decreed,
Concerning Bruno and the emperor,
In quittance of their late conspiracy
Against our state and papal dignity?

FAUSTUS

Most sacred patron of the church of Rome,
By full consent of all the synod
Of priests and prelates, it is thus decreed:
That Bruno, and the German emperor
Be held as lollards, and bold schismatics,
And proud disturbers of the church's peace.
And if that Bruno by his own assent,
Without enforcement of the German peers,
Did seek to wear the triple diadem,
And by your death to climb Saint Peter's chair,
The statutes decretal have thus decreed,
He shall be straight condemned of heresy,
And on a pile of faggots burned to death.

POPE

It is enough. Here, take him to your charge,
And bear him straight to Ponte Angelo,
And in the strongest tower enclose him fast.
Tomorrow, sitting in our consistory,
With all our college of grave cardinals,
We will determine of his life or death.
Here, take his triple crown along with you,
And leave it in the church's treasury.
Make haste again, my good lord cardinals,
And take our blessing apostolical.

MEPHOSTOPHILIS

So, so, was never devil thus blest before!

FAUSTUS

Away, sweet Mephostophilis, be gone!
The cardinals will be plagued for this anon.

Exeunt FAUSTUS *and* MEPHOSTOPHILIS

POPE

> Go presently, and bring a banquet forth,
> That we may solemnize Saint Peter's feast,
> And with Lord Raymond, King of Hungary,
> Drink to our late and happy victory.   *Exeunt*

> *A sennet while the banquet is brought in; and then enter*
> FAUSTUS *and* MEPHOSTOPHILIS *in their*
> *own shapes*

MEPHOSTOPHILIS

> Now Faustus, come prepare thyself for mirth;
> The sleepy cardinals are hard at hand,
> To censure Bruno, that is posted hence,
> And on a proud paced steed, as swift as thought,
> Flies o'er the alps to fruitful Germany,
> There to salute the woeful emperor.

FAUSTUS

> The pope will curse them for their sloth today
> That slept both Bruno and his crown away.
> But now, that Faustus may delight his mind,
> And by their folly make some merriment,
> Sweet Mephostophilis, so charm me here,
> That I may walk invisible to all,
> And do whate'er I please, unseen of any.

MEPHOSTOPHILIS

> Faustus thou shalt; then kneel down presently,
> *Whilst on thy head I lay my hand,*
> *And charm thee with this magic wand.*
> *First wear this girdle, then appear*
> *Invisible to all are here:*
> *The planets seven, the gloomy air,*
> *Hell, and the Fury's forked hair,*
> *Pluto's blue fire, and Hecate's tree,*
> *With magic spells so compass thee,*
> *That no eye may thy body see.*
> So Faustus, now for all their holiness,
> Do what thou wilt, thou shalt not be discerned.

FAUSTUS

> Thanks Mephostophilis; now friars, take heed
> Lest Faustus make your shaven crowns to bleed.

MEPHOSTOPHILIS
Faustus, no more: see where the cardinals come.

Enter POPE *and all the lords. Enter the* CARDINALS
with a book

POPE
Welcome lord cardinals: come sit down.
Lord Raymond, take your seat; friars, attend,
And see that all things be in readiness,
As beseems this solemn festival.

1 CARDINAL
First, may it please your sacred holiness
To view the sentence of the reverend synod,
Concerning Bruno and the emperor.

POPE
What needs this question? Did I not tell you,
Tomorrow we would sit i'th' consistory,
And there determine of his punishment?
You brought us word even now, it was decreed,
That Bruno and the cursed emperor
Were by the holy council both condemned
For loathed lollards, and base schismatics.
Then wherefore would you have me view that book?

1 CARDINAL
Your grace mistakes, you gave us no such charge.

RAYMOND
Deny it not, we are all witnesses
That Bruno here was late delivered you,
With his rich triple crown to be reserved
And put into the church's treasury.

AMBO CARDINALS
By holy Paul we saw them not.

POPE
By Peter you shall die,
Unless you bring them forth immediately:
Hale them to prison, lade their limbs with gyves!
False prelates, for this hateful treachery,
Cursed be your souls to hellish misery.

FAUSTUS
So, they are safe: now Faustus to the feast,
The pope had never such a frolic guest.

POPE

    Lord archbishop of Rheims, sit down with us.

BISHOP

    I thank your holiness.

FAUSTUS

    Fall to, the devil choke you an you spare.

POPE

    Who's that spoke? Friars, look about.

    Lord Raymond pray fall to; I am beholding

    To the bishop of Milan for this so rare a present.

FAUSTUS

    I thank you sir.

POPE

    How now? Who snatched the meat from me?

    Villains, why speak you not?

    My good lord archbishop, here's a most dainty dish,

    Was sent me from a cardinal in France.

FAUSTUS

    I'll have that too.

POPE

    What lollards do attend our holiness

    That we receive such great indignity? Fetch me some wine.

FAUSTUS

    Ay, pray do, for Faustus is a-dry.

POPE

    Lord Raymond, I drink unto your grace.

FAUSTUS

    I pledge your grace.

POPE

    My wine gone too? Ye lubbers, look about

    And find the man that doth this villainy,

    Or by our sanctitude you all shall die.

    I pray my lords, have patience at this

    Troublesome banquet.

BISHOP

    Please it your holiness, I think it be some ghost crept out of

    purgatory, and now is come unto your holiness for his pardon.

POPE

    It may be so:

    Go then command our priests to sing a dirge,

    To lay the fury of this same troublesome ghost.

FAUSTUS

    How now? Must every bit be spiced with a cross?

    Nay then, take that.

POPE

    O I am slain, help me my lords;

    O come and help to bear my body hence.

    Damned be this soul for ever, for this deed.

Exeunt the POPE *and his train*

MEPHOSTOPHILIS

    Now Faustus, what will you do now? for I can tell you

    You'll be cursed with bell, book and candle.

FAUSTUS

    Bell, book, and candle; candle, book, and bell:

    Forward and backward, to curse Faustus to hell.

Enter the FRIARS *with bell, book, and candle,*
for the dirge

1 FRIAR

    Come brethren, let's about our business with good devotion.

        Cursed be he that stole his holiness' meat from the table.

            Maledicat Dominus.

        Cursed be he that struck his holiness a blow [on] the face.

            Maledicat Dominus.

        Cursed be he that struck friar Sandelo a blow on the pate.

            Maledicat Dominus.

        Cursed be he that disturbeth our holy dirge.

            Maledicat Dominus.

        Cursed be he that took away his holiness' wine

            Maledicat Dominus.

Beat the friars, fling fireworks among them,
and exeunt

Exeunt

Scene 8

Enter CLOWN [ROBIN] *and* DICK, *with a cup*

DICK

    Sirra Robin, we were best look that your devil can answer the
    stealing of this same cup, for the vintner's boy follows us at the
    hard heels.

ROBIN

'Tis no matter, let him come; an he follow us, I'll so conjure him, as he was never conjured in his life, I warrant him. Let me see the cup.

Enter VINTNER

DICK

Here 'tis. Yonder he comes: now Robin, now or never show thy cunning.

VINTNER

O, are you here? I am glad I have found you, you are a couple of fine companions: pray where's the cup you stole from the tavern?

ROBIN

How, how? We steal a cup? Take heed what you say, we look not like cup-stealers, I can tell you.

VINTNER

Never deny't, for I know you have it, and I'll search you.

ROBIN

Search me? Ay, and spare not: hold the cup Dick – come, come, search me, search me.

VINTNER

Come on sirra, let me search you now.

DICK

Ay, ay; do, do. Hold the cup, Robin. I fear not your searching; we scorn to steal your cups, I can tell you.

VINTNER

Never outface me for the matter, for sure the cup is between you two.

ROBIN

Nay there you lie, 'tis beyond us both.

VINTNER

A plague take you, I thought 'twas your knavery to take it away. Come, give it me again.

ROBIN

Ay, much, when can you tell? Dick, make me a circle and stand close at my back, and stir not for thy life. Vintner, you shall have your cup anon – say nothing, Dick. *O per se o, demogorgon, Belcher* and *Mephostophilis.*

Enter MEPHOSTOPHILIS

MEPHOSTOPHILIS

You princely legions of infernal rule,
How am I vexed by these villains' charms?

From Constantinople have they brought me now,
Only for pleasure of these damned slaves.

ROBIN

By lady sir, you have had a shrewd journey of it! Will it please you
to take a shoulder of mutton to supper, and a tester in your purse,
and go back again?

DICK

Ay, I pray you heartily sir, for we called you but in jest, I promise
you.

MEPHOSTOPHILIS

To purge the rashness of this cursed deed,
First, be thou turned to this ugly shape,
For apish deeds transformed to an ape.

ROBIN

O brave, an ape? I pray sir, let me have the carrying of him about
to show some tricks.

MEPHOSTOPHILIS

And so thou shalt: be thou transformed to a dog, and carry him
upon thy back. Away, be gone.

ROBIN

A dog? That's excellent: let the maids look well to their porridge-
pots, for I'll into the kitchen presently. Come Dick, come.

Exeunt the two CLOWNS

MEPHOSTOPHILIS

Now with the flames of ever-burning fire,
I'll wing my self, and forthwith fly amain
Unto my Faustus, to the great Turk's court.   *Exit*

Scene 9

Enter MARTINO *and* FREDERICK *at several doors*

MARTINO

What ho, officers, gentlemen,
Hie to the presence to attend the emperor.
Good Frederick, see the rooms be voided straight;
His majesty is coming to the hall;
Go back, and see the state in readiness.

FREDERICK
    But where is Bruno, our elected pope,
    That on a Fury's back came post from Rome?
    Will not his grace consort the emperor?
MARTINO
    O yes; and with him comes the German conjuror,
    The learned Faustus, fame of Wittenberg,
    The wonder of the world for magic art.
    And he intends to show great Carolus
    The race of all his stout progenitors;
    And bring in presence of his majesty
    The royal shapes and warlike semblances
    Of Alexander and his beauteous paramour.
FREDERICK
    Where is Benvolio?
MARTINO
    Fast asleep, I warrant you;
    He took his rouse with stoops of Rhenish wine
    So kindly yesternight to Bruno's health,
    That all this day the sluggard keeps his bed.
FREDERICK
    See, see – his window's ope; we'll call to him.
MARTINO
    What ho, Benvolio!

                Enter BENVOLIO *above at a window,*
                        in his nightcap: buttoning
BENVOLIO
    What a devil ail you two?
MARTINO
    Speak softly sir, lest the devil hear you:
    For Faustus at the court is late arrived,
    And at his heels a thousand furies wait
    To accomplish whatsoever the doctor please.
BENVOLIO
    What of this?
MARTINO
    Come, leave thy chamber first, and thou shalt see
    This conjuror perform such rare exploits
    Before the pope and royal emperor,
    As never yet was seen in Germany.

BENVOLIO

    Has not the pope enough of conjuring yet?
    He was upon the devil's back late enough,
    And if he be so far in love with him,
    I would he would post with him to Rome again.

FREDERICK

    Speak, wilt thou come and see this sport?

BENVOLIO

    Not I.

MARTINO

    Wilt thou stand in thy window and see it then?

BENVOLIO

    Ay, and I fall not asleep i'th' meantime.

MARTINO

    The emperor is at hand, who comes to see
    What wonders by black spells may compassed be.

BENVOLIO

    Well, go you attend the emperor. I am content for this once to
    thrust my head out at a window – for they say, if a man be drunk
    overnight, the devil cannot hurt him in the morning. If that be
    true, I have a charm in my head, shall control him as well as the
    conjuror, I warrant you.

                                                  [Withdraws]

    A sennet. [Enter] CHARLES *the German emperor,* BRUNO,
        SAXONY, FAUSTUS, MEPHOSTOPHILIS,
                [to]
           FREDERICK, MARTINO,
           and Attendants

EMPEROR

    Wonder of men, renowned magician,
    Thrice learned Faustus, welcome to our court.
    This deed of thine, in setting Bruno free
    From his and our professed enemy,
    Shall add more excellence unto thine art
    Than if by powerful necromantic spells
    Thou couldst command the world's obedience:
    For ever be beloved of Carolus.
    And if this Bruno thou hast late redeemed
    In peace possess the triple diadem,
    And sit in Peter's chair, despite of chance,
    Thou shalt be famous through all Italy,

And honoured of the German emperor.

FAUSTUS

These gracious words, most royal Carolus,
Shall make poor Faustus to his utmost power
Both love and serve the German emperor,
And lay his life at holy Bruno's feet.
For proof whereof, if so your grace be pleased,
The doctor stands prepared, by power of art,
To cast his magic charms, that shall pierce through
The ebon gates of ever-burning hell,
And hale the stubborn Furies from their caves,
To compass whatso'er your grace commands.

BENVOLIO

'Blood, he speaks terribly! But for all that, I do not greatly believe
him: he looks as like conjuror as the pope to a costermonger.

EMPEROR

Then Faustus, as thou late didst promise us,
We would behold that famous conqueror,
Great Alexander, and his paramour,
In their true shapes and state majestical,
That we may wonder at their excellence.

FAUSTUS

Your majesty shall see them presently.
Mephostophilis, away,
And with a solemn noise of trumpets' sound,
Present before this royal emperor,
Great Alexander and his beauteous paramour.

MEPHOSTOPHILIS

Faustus I will.

BENVOLIO

Well master doctor, an your devils come not away quickly, you
shall have me asleep presently: zounds, I could eat myself for anger,
to think I have been such an ass all this while, to stand gaping after
the devil's governor, and can see nothing.

FAUSTUS

I'll make you feel something anon, if my art fail me not.
My lord, I must forewarn your majesty
That when my spirits present the royal shapes
Of Alexander and his paramour,
Your grace demand no questions of the king,
But in dumb silence let them come and go.

EMPEROR

Be it as Faustus please, we are content.

BENVOLIO

Ay, ay; and I am content too: and thou bring Alexander and his paramour before the emperor, I'll be Actaeon, and turn myself into a stag.

FAUSTUS

And I'll play Diana, and send you the horns presently.

Sennet. Enter at one [door] the emperor ALEXANDER, *at the other [door]* DARIUS; *they meet,* DARIUS *is thrown down,* ALEXANDER *kills him, takes off his crown, and offering to go out, his paramour meets him. He embraceth her, and sets Darius' crown upon her head; and coming back, both salute the emperor who, leaving his state, offers to embrace them, which* FAUSTUS *seeing, suddenly stays him. Then trumpets cease, and music sounds*

My gracious lord, you do forget yourself:
These are but shadows, not substantial.

EMPEROR

O pardon me, my thoughts are so ravished
With sight of this renowned emperor,
That in mine arms I would have compassed him.
But Faustus, since I may not speak to them,
To satisfy my longing thoughts at full,
Let me this tell thee: I have heard it said,
That this fair lady, whilst she lived on earth,
Had on her neck a little wart or mole;
How may I prove that saying to be true?

FAUSTUS

Your majesty may boldly go and see.

EMPEROR

Faustus, I see it plain!
And in this sight thou better pleasest me,
Than if I gained another monarchy.

FAUSTUS

Away, be gone.   *Exit Show*

See, see, my gracious lord, what strange beast is yon, that thrusts his head out at window.

EMPEROR

O wondrous sight: see, duke of Saxony,

Two spreading horns most strangely fastened
Upon the head of young Benvolio.

SAXONY

What, is he asleep – or dead?

FAUSTUS

He sleeps, my lord, but dreams not of his horns.

EMPEROR

This sport is excellent: we'll call and wake him.
What ho, Benvolio!

BENVOLIO

A plague upon you, let me sleep awhile.

EMPEROR

I blame thee not to sleep much, having such a head of thine
own.

SAXONY

Look up, Benvolio; 'tis the emperor calls.

BENVOLIO

The emperor! Where? O zounds, my head.

EMPEROR

Nay, and thy horns hold, 'tis no matter for thy head, for that's
armed sufficiently.

FAUSTUS

Why, how now sir knight, what hanged by the horns? This [is]
most horrible: fie, fie, pull in your head for shame, let not all the
world wonder at you.

BENVOLIO

Zounds, doctor, is this your villainy?

FAUSTUS

O say not so, sir: the doctor has no skill,
No art, no cunning, to present these lords,
Or bring before this royal emperor
The mighty monarch, warlike Alexander.
If Faustus do it, you are straight resolved
In bold Actaeon's shape to turn a stag.
And therefore, my lord – so please your majesty –
I'll raise a kennel of hounds shall hunt him so
As all his footmanship shall scarce prevail
To keep his carcass from their bloody fangs.
Ho, Belimoth, Argiron, Asteroth!

BENVOLIO

Hold, hold! Zounds, he'll raise up a kennel of devils, I think, anon.

Good my lord, entreat for me: 'sblood, I am never able to endure
these torments.

EMPEROR

Then, good master doctor,
Let me entreat you to remove his horns:
He has done penance now sufficiently.

FAUSTUS

My gracious lord, not so much for injury done to me, as to delight
your majesty with some mirth, hath Faustus justly requited this
injurious knight; which being all I desire, I am content to remove
his horns. Mephostophilis, transform him; and hereafter sir, look
you speak well of scholars.

BENVOLIO

Speak well of you? 'Sblood, and scholars be such cuckold-makers
to clap horns of honest men's heads o'this order. I'll ne'er trust
smooth faces and small ruffs more. But an I be not revenged for
this, would I might be turned to a gaping oyster and drink nothing
but salt water.   [*Exit*]

EMPEROR

Come Faustus; while the emperor lives,
In recompence of this thy high desert,
Thou shalt command the state of Germany,
And live beloved of mighty Carolus.

Exeunt omnes

Enter BENVOLIO, MARTINO, FREDERICK,
and Soldiers

MARTINO

Nay, sweet Benvolio, let us sway thy thoughts
From this attempt against the conjuror.

BENVOLIO

Away, you love me not to urge me thus.
Shall I let slip so great an injury,
When every servile groom jests at my wrongs,
And in their rustic gambols proudly say,
'Benvolio's head was graced with horns today'!
O may these eyelids never close again,
Till with my sword I have that conjuror slain.
If you will aid me in this enterprise,
Then draw your weapons, and be resolute:
If not, depart: here will Benvolio die –

But Faustus' death shall quit my infamy!

FREDERICK

Nay, we will stay with thee, betide what may,
And kill that doctor if he come this way.

BENVOLIO

Then gentle Frederick, hie thee to the grove,
And place our servants, and our followers
Close in an ambush there behind the trees;
By this (I know) the conjuror is near:
I saw him kneel, and kiss the emperor's hand,
And take his leave, laden with rich rewards.
Then soldiers, boldly fight; if Faustus die,
Take you the wealth, leave us the victory.

FREDERICK

Come soldiers, follow me unto the grove;
Who kills him shall have gold, and endless love.

Exit FREDERICK *with the* SOLDIERS

BENVOLIO

My head is lighter than it was by th'horns,
But yet my heart more ponderous than my head,
And pants until I see that conjuror dead.

MARTINO

Where shall we place ourselves Benvolio?

BENVOLIO

Here will we stay to bide the first assault.
O were that damned hellhound but in place,
Thou soon shouldst see me quit my foul disgrace.

Enter FREDERICK

FREDERICK

Close, close, the conjuror is at hand,
And, all alone, comes walking in his gown.
Be ready then, and strike the peasant down.

BENVOLIO

Mine be that honour then: now sword strike home,
For horns he gave, I'll have his head anon.

Enter FAUSTUS *with the false head*

MARTINO

See, see, he comes.

BENVOLIO

No words: this blow ends all!
Hell take his soul, his body thus must fall.

FAUSTUS

Oh.

FREDERICK

Groan you, master doctor?

BENVOLIO

Break may his heart with groans! Dear Frederick, see
Thus will I end his griefs immediately.

MARTINO

Strike with a willing hand, his head is off.

BENVOLIO

The devil's dead, the furies now may laugh.

FREDERICK

Was this that stern aspect, that awful frown,
Made the grim monarch of infernal spirits
Tremble and quake at his commanding charms?

MARTINO

Was this that damned head, whose heart conspired
Benvolio's shame before the emperor?

BENVOLIO

Ay that's the head, and here the body lies,
Justly rewarded for his villainies.

FREDERICK

Come, let's devise how we may add more shame
To the black scandal of his hated name.

BENVOLIO

First, on his head, in quittance of my wrongs,
I'll nail huge forked horns, and let them hang
Within the window where he yoked me first,
That all the world may see my just revenge.

MARTINO

What use shall we put his beard to?

BENVOLIO

We'll sell it to a chimney-sweeper: it will wear out ten birchen
brooms, I warrant you.

FREDERICK

What shall eyes do?

BENVOLIO

We'll put out his eyes, and they shall serve for buttons to his lips, to keep his tongue from catching cold.

MARTINO

An excellent policy! And now sirs, having divided him, what shall the body do?

[FAUSTUS *gets up*]

BENVOLIO

Zounds, the devil's alive again.

FREDERICK

Give him his head, for God's sake.

FAUSTUS

Nay keep it: Faustus will have heads and hands,
Ay, all your hearts to recompense this deed.
Knew you not, traitors, I was limited
For four-and-twenty years to breathe on earth?
And had you cut my body with your swords,
Or hew'd this flesh and bones as small as sand,
Yet in a minute had my spirit returned,
And I had breathed a man made free from harm.
But wherefore do I dally my revenge?
Asteroth, Belimoth, Mephostophilis.

Enter MEPHOSTOPHILIS *and other* DEVILS

Go, horse these traitors on your fiery backs,
And mount aloft with them as high as heaven,
Thence pitch them headlong to the lowest hell:
Yet stay, the world shall see their misery,
And hell shall after plague their treachery.
Go Belimoth, and take this caitiff hence,
And hurl him in some lake of mud and dirt;
Take thou this other, drag him through the woods,
Amongst the pricking thorns and sharpest briars,
Whilst with my gentle Mephostophilis,
This traitor flies unto some steepy rock,
That rolling down, may break the villain's bones,
As he intended to dismember me.
Fly hence, dispatch my charge immediately.

FREDERICK

Pity us, gentle Faustus, save our lives.

FAUSTUS

Away.

FREDERICK
  He must needs go that the devil drives.
                              Exeunt SPIRITS *with the* KNIGHTS

                    Enter the ambushed SOLDIERS

1 SOLDIER
  Come sirs, prepare yourselves in readiness,
  Make haste to help these noble gentlemen.
  I heard them parley with the conjuror.
2 SOLDIER
  See where he comes! Dispatch, and kill the slave.
FAUSTUS
  What's here? An ambush to betray my life!
  Then Faustus, try thy skill: base peasants stand,
  For lo, these trees remove at my command,
  And stand as bulwarks 'twixt yourselves and me,
  To shield me from your hated treachery!
  Yet to encounter this your weak attempt,
  Behold an army comes incontinent.

        FAUSTUS *strikes the door, and enter a* DEVIL *playing
        on a drum; after him another bearing an ensign; and
        divers with weapons;* MEPHOSTOPHILIS *with fireworks.
        They set upon the* SOLDIERS, *and drive them out*

      Enter at several doors BENVOLIO, FREDERICK, *and* MARTINO,
          *their heads and faces bloody, and besmeared with
              mud and dirt; all having horns on their heads*

MARTINO
  What ho, Benvolio!
BENVOLIO
  Here, what Frederick, ho!
FREDERICK
  O help me, gentle friend; where is Martino?
MARTINO
  Dear Frederick, here –
  Half smothered in a lake of mud and dirt,
  Through which the Furies dragged me by the heels.
FREDERICK
  Martino, see
  Benvolio's horns again!

MARTINO
O misery! How now Benvolio?

BENVOLIO
Defend me heaven, shall I be haunted still?

MARTINO
Nay fear not, man; we have no power to kill.

BENVOLIO
My friends transformed thus: O hellish spite,
Your heads are all set with horns.

FREDERICK   You hit it right,
It is your own you mean: feel on your head.

BENVOLIO
'Zounds, horns again!

MARTINO
Nay chafe not, man: we all are sped.

BENVOLIO
What devil attends this damned magician,
That spite of spite our wrongs are doubled?

FREDERICK
What may we do, that we may hide our shames?

BENVOLIO
If we should follow him to work revenge,

He'd join long asses' ears to these huge horns,
And make us laughing-stocks to all the world.

MARTINO
What shall we do then, dear Benvolio?

BENVOLIO
I have a castle joining near these woods,
And thither we'll repair, and live obscure
Till time shall alter this our brutish shapes.
Sith black disgrace hath thus eclipsed our fame,
We'll rather die with grief, than live with shame.

Exeunt omnes

Scene 10

Enter FAUSTUS *and the* HORSE-COURSER,
and MEPHOSTOPHILIS

HORSE-COURSER
I beseech your worship accept of these forty dollars.

FAUSTUS

Friend, thou canst not buy so good a horse, for so small a price: I
have no great need to sell him, but if thou likest him for ten dollars
more, take him, because I see thou hast a good mind to him.

HORSE-COURSER

I beseech you sir, accept of this; I am a very poor man, and have
lost very much of late by horseflesh, and this bargain will set me
up again.

FAUSTUS

Well, I will not stand with thee; give me the money. Now sirra I must
tell you, that you may ride him o'er hedge and ditch, and spare him
not; but, do you hear, in any case ride him not into the water.

HORSE-COURSER

How sir, not into the water? Why, will he not drink of all waters?

FAUSTUS

Yes, he will drink of all waters, but ride him not into the water:
o'er hedge and ditch, or where thou wilt, but not into the water.
Go bid the ostler deliver him unto you, and remember what I say.

HORSE-COURSER

I warrant you sir. O joyful day! Now am I a made man for ever.

Exit

FAUSTUS

What art thou, Faustus, but a man condemned to die?
Thy fatal time draws to a final end;
Despair doth drive distrust into my thoughts.
Confound these passions with a quiet sleep:
Tush, Christ did call the thief upon the cross,
Then rest thee, Faustus, quiet in conceit.

He sits to sleep

Enter the HORSE-COURSER *wet*

HORSE-COURSER

O what a cozening doctor was this! I riding my horse into the water,
thinking some hidden mystery had been in the horse, I had nothing
under me but a little straw, and had much ado to escape drowning!
Well, I'll go rouse him, and make him give me my forty dollars
again. Ho, sirra doctor, you cozening scab; master doctor awake,
and rise, and give me my money again, for your horse is turned to
a bottle of hay, – master doctor.

He pulls off his leg

Alas I am undone, what shall I do? I have pulled off his leg.

FAUSTUS

O help, help, the villain hath murdered me.

HORSE-COURSER

Murder or not murder, now he has but one leg, I'll out-run him, and cast this leg into some ditch or other.   *Exit*

FAUSTUS

Stop him, stop him, stop him – ha, ha, ha, Faustus hath his leg again, and the horse-courser a bundle of hay for his forty dollars.

Enter WAGNER

How now Wagner, what news with thee?

WAGNER

If it please you, the Duke of Vanholt doth earnestly entreat your company, and hath sent some of his men to attend you with provision fit for your journey.

FAUSTUS

The Duke of Vanholt's an honourable gentleman, and one to whom I must be no niggard of my cunning. Come away.

Exeunt

Scene 10b

[This scene is found only the B Text, where it is inserted after Wagner's announcement of the Duke of Vanholt's invitation.]

Enter CLOWN [ROBIN], DICK, HORSE-COURSER *and a*
CARTER

CARTER

Come, my masters, I'll bring you to the best beer in Europe. What ho, hostess, where be these whores?

Enter HOSTESS

HOSTESS

How now, what lack you? What, my old guests, welcome.

ROBIN

Sirra Dick, dost thou know why I stand so mute?

DICK

No Robin, why is't?

ROBIN

I am eighteen pence on the score, but say nothing, see if she have forgotten me.

HOSTESS

Who's this, that stands so solemnly by himself? What, my old guest?

ROBIN

O hostess, how do you? I hope my score stands still.

HOSTESS

Ay, there's no doubt of that, for methinks you make no haste to wipe it out.

DICK

Why hostess, I say, fetch us some beer.

HOSTESS

You shall presently: look up into th'hall there, ho!   *Exit*

DICK

Come sirs, what shall we do now till mine hostess comes?

CARTER

Marry sir, I'll tell you the bravest tale how a conjuror served me; you know Doctor Fauster?

HORSE-COURSER

Ay, a plague take him! Here's some on's have cause to know him; did he conjure thee too?

CARTER

I'll tell you how he served me. As I was going to Wittenberg t'other day, with a load of hay, he met me, and asked me what he should give me for as much hay as he could eat; now sir, I thinking that a little would serve his turn, bade him take as much as he would for three-farthings; so he presently gave me my money, and fell to eating; and as I am a christen man, he never left eating, till he had ate up all my load of hay.

ALL

O monstrous, eat a whole load of hay!

ROBIN

Yes, yes, that may be; for I have heard of one, that ha's ate a load of logs.

HORSE-COURSER

Now sirs, you shall hear how villainously he served me: I went to him yesterday to buy a horse of him, and he would by no means sell him under forty dollars; so sir, because I knew him to be such a horse, as would run over hedge and ditch, and never tire, I gave him his money; so when I had my horse, Doctor Fauster bade me ride him night and day, and spare him no time; but, quoth he, in any case ride him not into the water. Now sir, I thinking the horse had had some quality that he would not have me know of, what did I but rid him into a great river, and when I came just in the midst my horse vanished away, and I sat straddling upon a bottle of hay.

ALL

O brave, doctor!

HORSE-COURSER

But you shall hear how bravely I served him for it. I went me home to his house, and there I found him asleep. I kept a hallowing and whooping in his ears, but all could not wake him: I, seeing that, took him by the leg, and never rested pulling, till I had pulled me his leg quite off, and now 'tis at home in mine hostry.

ROBIN

And has the doctor but one leg then? That's excellent, for one of his devils turned me into the likeness of an ape's face.

CARTER

Some more drink, hostess.

ROBIN

Hark you, we'll into another room and drink awhile, and then we'll go seek out the doctor.   *Exeunt omnes*

Scene 11

Enter the DUKE *of Vanholt; his* DUCHESS,
FAUSTUS, *and* MEPHOSTOPHILIS

DUKE

Thanks, master doctor, for these pleasant sights; nor know I how sufficiently to recompense your great deserts in erecting that enchanted castle in the air; the sight whereof so delighted me, as nothing in the world could please me more.

FAUSTUS

I do think myself, my good lord, highly recompensed, in that it pleaseth your grace to think but well of that which Faustus hath performed. But, gracious lady, it may be, that you have taken no pleasure in those sights; therefore I pray

you tell me, what is the thing you most desire to have: be it
in the world, it shall be yours. I have heard that great-
bellied women do long for things are rare and dainty.

DUCHESS

True, master doctor; and since I find you so kind I will make known
unto you what my heart desires to have; and were it now summer,
as it is January, a dead time of the winter, I would request no better
meat, than a dish of ripe grapes.

FAUSTUS

This is but a small matter: go Mephostophilis; away!

Exit MEPHOSTOPHILIS

Madam, I will do more than this for your content.

Enter MEPHOSTOPHILIS *again with the grapes*

Here now taste ye these: they should be good
For they come from a far country, I can tell you.

DUKE

This makes me wonder more than all the rest, that at this time of
the year, when every tree is barren of his fruit, from whence you
had these ripe grapes.

FAUSTUS

Please it your grace, the year is divided into two circles over the
whole world, so that when it is winter with us, in the contrary circle
it is likewise summer with them, as in India, Saba, and such
countries that lie far east, where they have fruit twice a year. From
whence, by means of a swift spirit that I have, I had these grapes
brought as you see.

DUCHESS

And trust me, they are the sweetest grapes that e'er I tasted.

The CLOWNS [ROBIN, DICK, CARTER, HORSE-COURSER]
bounce at the gate, within

DUKE

What rude disturbers have we at the gate?
Go pacify their fury, set it ope,
And then demand of them, what they would have.

They knock again, and call out to talk with FAUSTUS
[*within*]

A SERVANT

Why how now masters, what a coil is there?

What is the reason you disturb the duke?

DICK

We have no reason for it, therefore a fig for him.

SERVANT

Why saucy varlets, dare you be so bold?

HORSE-COURSER

I hope sir, we have wit enough to be more bold than welcome.

SERVANT

It appears so. Pray be bold elsewhere,
And trouble not the duke.

DUKE

What would they have?

SERVANT

They all cry out to speak with Doctor Faustus.

CARTER

Ay, and we will speak with him.

DUKE

Will you sir? Commit the rascals.

DICK

Commit with us! He were as good commit with his father, as commit with us.

FAUSTUS

I do beseech your grace let them come in,
They are good subject for a merriment.

DUKE

Do as thou wilt Faustus, I give thee leave.

FAUSTUS

I thank your grace:

Enter [ROBIN], DICK, CARTER, *and* HORSE-COURSER

Why, how now, my good friends?
'Faith you are too outrageous, but come near,
I have procured your pardons: welcome all.

ROBIN

Nay sir, we will be welcome for our money, and we will pay for what we take. What ho, give's half a dozen of beer here, and be hanged.

FAUSTUS

Nay, hark you, can you tell me where you are?

CARTER

Ay, marry can I, we are under heaven.

SERVANT

Ay; but, sir sauce-box, know you in what place?

HORSE-COURSER

Ay, ay: the house is good enough to drink in. Zounds, fill us some beer, or we'll break all the barrels in the house, and dash out all your brains with your bottles.

FAUSTUS

Be not so furious: come, you shall have beer.

My Lord, beseech you give me leave awhile,

I'll gage my credit, 'twill content your grace.

DUKE

With all my heart, kind doctor; please thyself,

Our servants, and our court's at thy command.

FAUSTUS

I humbly thank your grace: then fetch some beer.

HORSE-COURSER

Ay, marry; there spake a doctor indeed – and 'faith I'll drink a health to thy wooden leg for that word.

FAUSTUS

My wooden leg? what dost thou mean by that?

CARTER

Ha, ha, ha, dost hear him Dick? He has forgot his leg.

HORSE-COURSER

Ay, ay, he does not stand much upon that.

FAUSTUS

No 'faith, not much upon a wooden leg.

CARTER

Good Lord, that flesh and blood should be so frail with your worship! Do not you remember a horse-courser you sold a horse to?

FAUSTUS

Yes, I remember I sold one a horse.

CARTER

And do you remember you bid he should not ride into the water?

FAUSTUS

Yes, I do very well remember that.

CARTER

And do you remember nothing of your leg?

FAUSTUS

No, in good sooth.

CARTER

Then I pray remember your courtesy.

FAUSTUS [*bowing*]

I thank you sir.

CARTER

'Tis not so much worth; I pray you tell me one thing.

FAUSTUS

What's that?

CARTER

Be both your legs bedfellows every night together?

FAUSTUS

Wouldst thou make a colossus of me, that thou askest me such questions?

CARTER

No, truly sir, I would make nothing of you, but I would fain know that.

Enter HOSTESS *with drink*

FAUSTUS

Then I assure thee certainly they are.

CARTER

I thank you; I am fully satisfied.

FAUSTUS

But wherefore dost thou ask?

CARTER

For nothing sir: but methinks you should have a wooden bedfellow of one of 'em.

HORSE-COURSER

Why, do you hear sir, did not I pull off one of your legs when you were asleep?

FAUSTUS

But I have it again now I am awake: look you here, sir.

ALL

O horrible! Had the doctor three legs?

CARTER

Do you remember sir, how you cozened me and eat up my load of –

FAUSTUS *charms him dumb*

DICK

Do you remember how you made me wear an ape's –

HORSE-COURSER

You whoreson conjuring scab, do you remember how you cozened
me with a ho –

ROBIN

Ha' you forgotten me? You think to carry it away with your hey-
pass and re-pass: do you remember the dog's fa –

Exeunt CLOWNS

HOSTESS

Who pays for the ale – hear you, master doctor, now you have sent
away my guests. I pray who shall pay me for my a –

Exit HOSTESS

DUCHESS

My lord,
We are much beholding to this learned man.

DUKE

So are we madam, which we will recompense
With all the love and kindness that we may:
His artful sport drives all sad thoughts away.   *Exeunt*

Scene 12

Thunder and lightning. Enter DEVILS *with covered dishes;*
MEPHOSTOPHILIS *leads them into* FAUSTUS' *study*
Then enter WAGNER

WAGNER

I think my master means to die shortly. He has made his will, and
given me his wealth, his house, his goods, and store of golden
plate, besides two thousand ducats ready coined: I wonder what he
means? If death were nigh, he would not frolic thus: he's now at
supper with the scholars, where there's such belly-cheer, as Wagner
in his life ne'er saw the like! And see where they come, belike the feast
is done.   *Exit*

Enter FAUSTUS, MEPHOSTOPHILIS, *and two or three*
SCHOLARS

1 SCHOLAR

Master doctor Faustus, since our conference about fair ladies, which
was the beautifullest in all the world, we have determined

[127]

with ourselves, that Helen of Greece was the admirablest lady that
ever lived: therefore master doctor, if you will do us so much
favour, as to let us see that peerless dame of Greece, whom all the
world admires for majesty, we should think ourselves much beholding
unto you.

FAUSTUS

Gentlemen, for that I know your friendship is unfained,
It is not Faustus' custom to deny
The just request of those that wish him well:
You shall behold that peerless dame of Greece,
No otherwise for pomp or majesty,
Than when sir Paris crossed the seas with her,
And brought the spoils to rich Dardania.
Be silent then, for danger is in words.

Music sound. MEPHOSTOPHILIS *brings in* HELEN;
she passeth over the stage

2 SCHOLAR

Was this fair Helen, whose admired worth
Made Greece with ten years' war afflict poor Troy?

3 SCHOLAR

Too simple is my wit to tell her worth,
Whom all the world admires for majesty.

1 SCHOLAR

Now we have seen the pride of Nature's work,
We'll take our leaves, and for this blessed sight
Happy and blest be Faustus evermore.

Exeunt SCHOLARS

FAUSTUS

Gentlemen farewell: the same wish I to you.

Enter an OLD MAN

OLD MAN

O gentle Faustus, leave this damned art,
This magic, that will charm thy soul to hell,
And quite bereave thee of salvation.
Though thou hast now offended like a man,
Do not persevere in it like a devil.
Yet, yet, thou hast an amiable soul,
If sin by custom grow not into nature.
Then Faustus, will repentance come too late,

Then thou art banished from the sight of heaven.
No mortal can express the pains of hell!
It may be this my exhortation
Seems harsh, and all unpleasant; let it not,
For, gentle son, I speak it not in wrath,
Or envy of thee, but in tender love,
And pity of thy future misery.
And so have hope, that this my kind rebuke,
Checking thy body, may amend thy soul.

FAUSTUS

Where art thou, Faustus? wretch, what hast thou done?
Hell claims his right, and with a roaring voice,

MEPHOSTOPHILIS *gives him a dagger*

Says 'Faustus, come: thine hour is almost come';
And Faustus now will come to do thee right.

OLD MAN

O stay, good Faustus, stay thy desperate steps.
I see an angel hover o'er thy head,
And with a vial full of precious grace,
OVers to pour the same into thy soul!
Then call for mercy, and avoid despair.

FAUSTUS

O friend, I feel thy words to comfort my distressed soul!
Leave me awhile, to ponder on my sins.

OLD MAN

Faustus I leave thee, but with grief of heart,
Fearing the enemy of thy hapless soul.   *Exit*

FAUSTUS

Accursed Faustus, wretch, what hast thou done?
I do repent, and yet I do despair,
Hell strives with grace for conquest in my breast:
What shall I do to shun the snares of death?

MEPHOSTOPHILIS

Thou traitor Faustus, I arrest thy soul
For disobedience to my sovereign lord.
Revolt, or I'll in piecemeal tear thy flesh . . .

[From this point the two texts coincide, except that B omits the
final appearance (and speech) of the Old Man.]

Scene 13

Thunder. Enter LUCIFER, BELZEBUB, *and* MEPHOSTOPHILIS

LUCIFER
Thus from infernal Dis do we ascend
To view the subjects of our monarchy,
Those souls which sin seals the black sons of hell.
'Mong which as chief, Faustus, we come to thee,
Bringing with us lasting damnation
To wait upon thy soul; the time is come
Which makes it forfeit.
MEPHOSTOPHILIS   And this gloomy night,
Here in this room will wretched Faustus be.
BELZEBUB
And here we'll stay,
To mark him how he doth demean himself.
MEPHOSTOPHILIS
How should he, but in desperate lunacy.
Fond worldling, now his heart-blood dries with grief;
His conscience kills it, and his labouring brain
Begets a world of idle fantasies,
To overreach the devil. But all in vain:
His store of pleasures must be sauced with pain.
He and his servant Wagner are at hand,
Both come from drawing Faustus' latest will.
See where they come.

Enter FAUSTUS *and* WAGNER

FAUSTUS
Say, Wagner, thou hast perused my will,
How dost thou like it?
WAGNER   Sir, so wondrous well,
As in all humble duty, I do yield
My life and lasting service for your love.

Enter the SCHOLARS

FAUSTUS
Gramercies Wagner. Welcome gentlemen.
1 SCHOLAR
Now worthy Faustus, methinks your looks are changed.

FAUSTUS

O gentlemen!

2 SCHOLAR

What ails Faustus?

FAUSTUS

Ah my sweet chamber-fellow, had I lived with thee,
Then had I lived still, but now must die eternally.
Look sirs, comes he not, comes he not?

1 SCHOLAR

O my dear Faustus, what imports this fear?

2 SCHOLAR

Is all our pleasure turned to melancholy?

3 SCHOLAR

He is not well with being over-solitary.

2 SCHOLAR

If it be so, we'll have physicians, and Faustus shall be cured.

3 SCHOLAR

'Tis but a surfeit sir, fear nothing.

FAUSTUS

A surfeit of deadly sin, that hath damned both body and soul.

3 SCHOLAR

Yet Faustus, look up to heaven, and remember mercy is infinite.

FAUSTUS

But Faustus' offence can ne'er be pardoned!
The serpent that tempted Eve may be saved,
But not Faustus. O gentlemen, hear with patience, and tremble
not at my speeches, though my heart pant and quiver to
remember that I have been a student here these thirty years – O
would I had never seen Wittenberg, never read book; and
what wonders I have done, all Germany can witness – yea, all
the world – for which Faustus hath lost both Germany and
the world – yea, heaven itself, heaven, the seat of God, the throne
of the blessed, the kingdom of joy; and must remain in hell
for ever. Hell, O hell for ever. Sweet friends, what shall become
of Faustus being in hell for ever?

2 SCHOLAR

Yet Faustus call on God.

FAUSTUS

On God, whom Faustus hath abjured? On God, whom Faustus
hath blasphemed! O my God, I would weep, but the devil draws
in my tears. Gush forth blood instead of tears, yea life and soul: O,

he stays my tongue: I would lift up my hands, but see they hold
'em, they hold 'em.

ALL

Who Faustus?

FAUSTUS

Why, Lucifer and Mephostophilis!
O gentlemen, I gave them my soul for my cunning.

ALL

O God forbid.

FAUSTUS

God forbade it indeed, but Faustus hath done it: for the vain
pleasure of four-and-twenty years hath Faustus lost eternal joy
and felicity. I writ them a bill with mine own blood, the date is
expired: this is the time, and he will fetch me.

1 SCHOLAR

Why did not Faustus tell us of this before, that divines might have
prayed for thee?

FAUSTUS

Oft have I thought to have done so: but the devil threatened to
tear me in pieces if I named God: to fetch me body and soul, if I
once gave ear to divinity: and now 'tis too late. Gentlemen away,
lest you perish with me.

2 SCHOLAR

O what may we do to save Faustus?

FAUSTUS

Talk not of me, but save yourselves and depart.

3 SCHOLAR

God will strengthen me; I will stay with Faustus.

1 SCHOLAR

Tempt not God, sweet friend, but let us into the next room, and
pray for him.

FAUSTUS

Ay, pray for me, pray for me: and what noise soever you hear, come
not unto me, for nothing can rescue me.

2 SCHOLAR

Pray thou, and we will pray, that God may have mercy upon thee.

FAUSTUS

Gentlemen farewell. If I live till morning, I'll visit you: if not,
Faustus is gone to hell.

ALL

Faustus, farewell.   *Exeunt* SCHOLARS

MEPHOSTOPHILIS

Ay, Faustus, now thou hast no hope of heaven,
Therefore despair, think only upon hell;
For that must be thy mansion, there to dwell.

FAUSTUS

O thou bewitching fiend, 'twas thy temptation
Hath robbed me of eternal happiness.

MEPHOSTOPHILIS

I do confess it Faustus, and rejoice!
'Twas I, that when thou wer't i'the way to heaven,
Dam'd up thy passage; when thou took'st the book
To view the Scriptures, then I turned the leaves
And led thine eye.
What weep'st thou? 'Tis too late; despair; farewell.
Fools that will laugh on earth, must weep in hell.   *Exit*

Enter the GOOD ANGEL *and the* BAD ANGEL
at several doors

GOOD ANGEL

O Faustus, if thou hadst given ear to me,
Innumerable joys had followed thee.
But thou didst love the world.

BAD ANGEL   Gave ear to me,
And now must taste hell's pains perpetually.

GOOD ANGEL

O what will all thy riches, pleasures, pomps,
Avail thee now?

BAD ANGEL   Nothing but vex thee more,
To want in hell, that had on earth such store.

Music while the throne descends

GOOD ANGEL

O thou has lost celestial happiness,
Pleasures unspeakable, bliss without end.
Hadst thou affected sweet divinity,
Hell, or the devil, had had no power on thee.
Hadst thou kept on that way, Faustus behold,
In what resplendent glory thou hadst sat
In yonder throne, like those bright shining saints,
And triumphed over hell: that hast thou lost,
And now poor soul must thy good angel leave thee,

The jaws of hell are open to receive thee.   *Exit*

Hell is discovered

BAD ANGEL

Now Faustus, let thine eyes with horror stare
Into that vast perpetual torture-house.
There are the Furies tossing damned souls,
On burning forks; there, bodies boil in lead.
There are live quarters broiling on the coals,
That ne'er can die! This ever-burning chair
Is for o'er-tortured souls to rest them in.
These, that are fed with sops of flaming fire,
Were gluttons, and loved only delicates,
And laughed to see the poor starve at their gates.
But yet all these are nothing. Thou shalt see
Ten thousand tortures that more horrid be.

FAUSTUS

O, I have seen enough to torture me.

BAD ANGEL

Nay, thou must feel them, taste the smart of all.
He that loves pleasure, must for pleasure fall:
And so I leave thee Faustus till anon,
Then wilt thou tumble in confusion.   *Exit*

The clock strikes eleven

FAUSTUS

O Faustus,
Now hast thou but one bare hour to live,
And then thou must be damned perpetually.
Stand still, you ever moving spheres of heaven,
That time may cease, and midnight never come.
Fair Nature's eye, rise, rise again and make
Perpetual day: or let this hour be but a year,
A month, a week, a natural day,
That Faustus may repent, and save his soul.
O lente lente currite noctis equi!
The stars move still, time runs, the clock will strike.
The devil will come, and Faustus must be damned.
O I'll leap up to heaven: who pulls me down?
One drop of blood will save me; O my Christ,
Rend not my heart for naming of my Christ.

Yet will I call on him: O spare me Lucifer.
Where is it now? 'Tis gone.
And see a threatening arm, an angry brow.
Mountains and hills, come, come, and fall on me,
And hide me from the heavy wrath of heaven.
No? Then will I headlong run into the earth:
Gape earth! O no, it will not harbour me.
You stars that reigned at my nativity,
Whose influence hath allotted death and hell,
Now draw up Faustus like a foggy mist,
Into the entrails of yon labouring cloud,
That when you vomit forth into the air,
My limbs may issue from your smoky mouths,
But let my soul mount, and ascend to heaven.

The watch strikes

O half the hour is past: 'twill all be past anon!
O, if my soul must suffer for my sin.
Impose some end to my incessant pain!
Let Faustus live in hell a thousand years,
A hundred thousand, and at last be saved.
No end is limited to damned souls.
Why wert thou not a creature wanting soul?
Or why is this immortal that thou hast?
O Pythagoras' *metempsychosis* – were that true,
This soul should fly from me, and I be changed
Into some brutish beast.
All beasts are happy, for when they die,
Their souls are soon dissolved in elements,
But mine must live still to be plagued in hell.
Cursed be the parents that engendered me;
No Faustus, curse thyself, curse Lucifer,
That hath deprived thee of the joys of heaven.

The clock strikes twelve

It strikes, it strikes! Now body, turn to air,
Or Lucifer will bear thee quick to hell.
O soul be changed into small water drops,
And fall into the ocean, ne'er be found.

Thunder, and enter the DEVILS

O mercy heaven, look not so fierce on me;
Adders and serpents, let me breathe awhile!
Ugly hell, gape not! Come not Lucifer!
I'll burn my books! O Mephostophilis!   *Exeunt*

[An additional scene, inserted between the final Soliloquy and the
Epilogue.]

Scene 13+

Enter the SCHOLARS

1 SCHOLAR

Come gentlemen, let us go visit Faustus,
For such a dreadful night was never seen
Since first the world's creation did begin.
Such fearful shrieks and cries were never heard!
Pray heaven the doctor have escaped the danger.

2 SCHOLAR

O help us heaven! See, here are Faustus' limbs,
All torn asunder by the hand of death.

3 SCHOLAR

The devils whom Faustus served have torn him thus!
For 'twixt the hours of twelve and one, methought
I heard hm shriek and call aloud for help:
At which self time the house seemed all on fire
With dreadful horror of these damned fiends.

2 SCHOLAR

Well gentlemen, tho' Faustus' end be such
As every Christian heart laments to think on,
Yet, for he was a scholar, once admired
For wondrous knowledge in our German schools,
We'll give his mangled limbs due burial.
And all the students, clothed in mourning black,
Shall wait upon his heavy funeral.   *Exeunt*

The Tragicall Histo⌐
of the Life and Death
of Doctor FAVSTVS.

With new Additions.

Written by *Ch. Mar.*

Printed at London for *Iohn Wright*, and are to be fold at his fhop without Newgate, 1624.